# TABLES
## You Can Customize

# TABLES
## You Can Customize

**ERNIE CONOVER**

**BETTERWAY BOOKS**

Cincinnati, Ohio

Other fine Betterway Books are available from your local bookstore or direct from the publisher.

00   99   98   97   96      5   4   3   2   1

Library of Congress Cataloging-in-Publication Data

Conover, Ernie.
    Tables you can customize/by Ernie Conover.
        p.   cm.—(Betterway woodworking plans series)
    Includes index
    ISBN 1-55870-397-7   (pbk.: alk. paper)
    1. Tables—Design and construction.   2. Woodwork   I. Title.
    II. Series.
TT197.5.T3C66   1996
684.1'3—dc20                    95-43657
                            CIP

Editor: Adam Blake
Production editor: Bruce E. Stoker
Interior designer: Brian Roeth
Cover designer: Sandy Kent
Illustrator: Bob Shreve
Photography: Ernie Conover

Betterway Books are available for sales promotions, premiums and fund-raising use. Special editions or book excerpts can also be created to specification. For details, contact the Special Sales Manager, F&W Publications, 1507 Dana Avenue, Cincinnati, Ohio 45207.

# DEDICATION

I would like to dedicate this book to my mentors, the first of whom has to be my father. His patient guidance has shaped me as a craftsman. More specifically, however, this book is dedicated to the mentors I have never met. In today's world the marvels of books and video make it possible to have greatly influential mentors who one has never met personally. I have gained much from the books of the following teachers. First was Charles H. Hayward whose books could always be found on my father's shelves when I was a boy. Second is Tage Frid whose books and articles have given me so much. I actually had the privilege of sitting next to Tage at a dinner several years ago and found him to be as charming in person as in print. I have gained much as an adult from Robert Wearing who caused me to re-focus on fundamentals. His book *The Essential Woodworker* is a must read for every wood craftsman. Finally there is Earnest Joyce. His seminal book *The Encyclopedia of Furniture Making* always solves the most difficult of problems.

# ACKNOWLEDGMENT

I would like to acknowledge the following friends and colleagues who were most helpful with information and tireless in reviewing text. Mike Dunbar (mortise and tenon joinery), Boyd Hutchison (wood movement), Jeff Jewitt (finishing), Bill Kaiser of Rochester Institute of Technology's School of American Craftsmen (mortise and tenon joinery), Kelly Mehler (general table construction), and Mark Schiefer of Delta International Machinery Corp. (machinery).

# ABOUT THE AUTHOR

Ernie Conover is an accomplished woodworker, author and workshop instructor—and world-reknowned expert on wood turning. He regularly publishes articles in woodworking magazines and is also the author of *The Lathe Book* and *The Router Table Book.* He lives in Parkman, Ohio.

## Read This Important Safety Notice

To prevent accidents, keep safety in mind while you work. Use the safety guards installed on power equipment; they are for your protection. When working on power equipment, keep fingers away from saw blades, wear safety goggles to prevent injuries from flying wood chips and sawdust, wear ear protection to protect your hearing, and consider installing a dust vacuum to reduce the amount of airborne sawdust in your woodshop. Don't wear loose clothing, such as neckties or shirts with loose sleeves, or jewelry, such as rings, necklaces or bracelets, when working on power equipment, and tie back long hair to prevent it from getting caught in your equipment. People who are sensitive to certain chemicals should check the chemical content of any product before using it. The author and editors who compiled this book have tried to make all the contents as accurate and correct as possible. Plans, illustrations, photographs and text have been carefully checked. All instructions, plans and projects should be carefully read, studied and understood before beginning construction. Due to the variability of local conditions, construction materials, skill levels, etc., neither the authors nor Betterway Books assumes any responsibility for any accidents, injuries, damages or other losses incurred resulting from the material presented in this book.

**Note:** Some photos show equipment being used with safety devices removed or moved out of the way for clarity.

| METRIC CONVERSION CHART | | |
|---|---|---|
| **TO CONVERT** | **TO** | **MULTIPLY BY** |
| Inches | Centimeters | 2.54 |
| Centimeters | Inches | 0.4 |
| Feet | Centimeters | 30.5 |
| Centimeters | Feet | 0.03 |
| Yards | Meters | 0.9 |
| Meters | Yards | 1.1 |
| Sq. Inches | Sq. Centimeters | 6.45 |
| Sq. Centimeters | Sq. Inches | 0.16 |
| Sq. Feet | Sq. Meters | 0.09 |
| Sq. Meters | Sq. Feet | 10.8 |
| Sq. Yards | Sq. Meters | 0.8 |
| Sq. Meters | Sq. Yards | 1.2 |
| Pounds | Kilograms | 0.45 |
| Kilograms | Pounds | 2.2 |
| Ounces | Grams | 28.4 |
| Grams | Ounces | 0.04 |

# Part One: Projects

Here are designs, dimensions and construction steps for you to build the end table, coffee table or dining table of your choice.

# Part Two: Techniques

Use the techniques explained in these chapters to customize your tables.

Take your basic table designs and customize the design with various leg styles: turned, tapered and cabriole.

Learn how to make the sturdiest table by building the sturdiest apron. Adapt the apron to hold a drawer or to release the legs quickly with knock-down hardware.

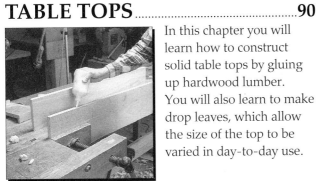

In this chapter you will learn how to construct solid table tops by gluing up hardwood lumber. You will also learn to make drop leaves, which allow the size of the top to be varied in day-to-day use.

Keep your flatware in a custom-built drawer, or keep your cards handy for that impromptu game. Learn how to make drawers and install them using store-bought hardware and home-made drawer pulls.

Make sure your table lasts and retains its good looks by finishing it with these techniques.

# Design and Build Your Own Tables with Confidence

*By using figured wood and turned legs this simple end table becomes an elegant heirloom.*

Only a chair is a more basic piece of furniture than a table. Any house needs many in a variety of heights and sizes—coffee tables, end tables, dining tables and work tables are all essential to every day life. While a chair is rather complicated to make, a table is really quite easy and makes a good basic woodworking project. Even a large dining table can be made in rather short time. What is more, the finest of materials and workmanship can be employed in our shop-built table, while the average store-bought example often proves rather shoddy. Present day store-bought furniture is seldom made entirely of solid wood and is often assembled with inferior joinery. When one recovers from the sticker shock of such store-bought tables, building your own becomes not just a viable option but an economic tour de force. That the resulting table can be made with solid wood construction, employing exceptional wood and joinery, is the pièce de résistance.

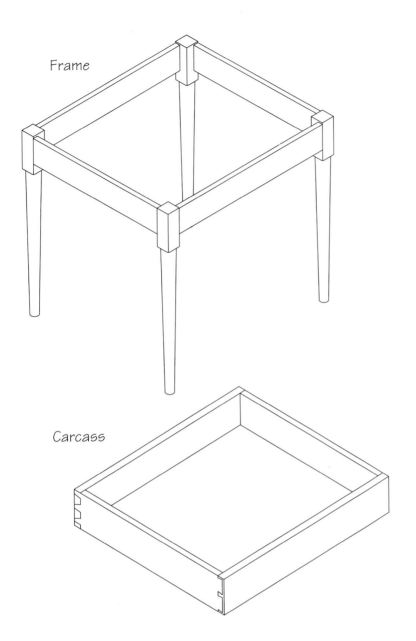

Frame

Carcass

# BUILDING TABLES

All furniture is either of carcass or frame construction or in some cases a combination of the two. Tables are pure frame construction. The legs and the aprons form the frame which supports the top. The frame may also support one or more drawers, which, interestingly enough, are pure carcass construction.

The best way to tackle a complex problem is to break it into small parts and tackle each independently. By resolving each part in turn, the entire problem is solved in short order. Building a table is just such a problem. In the following chapters we will take a closer look at the parts of a table and how they go together. The resulting information will allow us to build any table with confidence. This book is meant to be a study guide for the beginner as well as an encyclopedia of table building techniques that the accomplished furniture maker can consult when faced with problems.

# PART ONE

# PROJECTS

# CHAPTER ONE

# MAKING END TABLES

*This beautiful Early American end table is just one of the four end table designs you will find in this chapter.*

End tables are a great project to make if you are new to woodworking. They are relatively easy to make, they do not require a lot of lumber, and they are a great way to hone a variety of woodworking skills. I offer four designs here that are representative of four different furniture styles. See pages 8,9 for line drawings of the style variations. With no trouble at all you should be able to match existing furniture in your home with one of these tables, or you could begin to furnish your entire house starting with a table you make here!

# EARLY AMERICAN END TABLE

Early American furniture is actually a wide grouping of similar styles covering more than 100 years of early American history. The vast majority of furniture styles in this grouping were influenced heavily by European designs. As many craftsmen brought along furniture making styles from their homeland, American furniture had a resemblance to the reigning styles of the time.

Although it was constructed by craftsmen who built furniture according to European styles, early American furniture had its own characteristics. One of the main causes of the difference in styles was the separation from Europe by the Atlantic Ocean, followed closely by the eventual westward expansion of America. As the physical gap grew, the time periods for similar styles overlapped; for example, William and Mary styles of America were behind the William and Mary style of England by about twenty years. Another result of this is the noticeable difference in design; while its European counterparts exhibited intricate flourishes and details, early American furniture was much more plain in design and detail.

Early American furniture also varied with regional characteristics in influence and materials. For example, furniture of New England and some of the southern Middle Atlantic regions were mostly influenced by English style, while furniture from New York exhibited a Dutch influence and from New Orleans a French influence. Likewise, region dictated the materials used in furniture making; New England styles were known for pieces made from walnut, cherry and maple, while pieces from New York and Philadelphia were made from walnut and imported mahogany.

Regardless of the time span in which one particular early American style developed, the primary characteristics were simplicity and practicality. Simplicity of style and construction were dictated by the available tools and materials of the New World. Simplicity was also dictated by the pragmatism of colonial Americans; simple construction made for furniture that was built quickly and moved easily.

This table is based on an antique that has been in our family for many years. The original is a country piece made of tulip poplar. It has always been a favorite with everyone, but most of us wish it had been made from better wood. Therefore, I structured the table for my hand tool joinery class one year. It was successful, so I used it as the machine tool joinery project the next year. Many of my students acquired a pair of these lovely tables in this way. To make the turning more doable for a neophyte, I broadened the two beads just below the pommel and moved them down from the shoulder a bit. Other than this detail, it is a reproduction of the original. I made a set of bedroom tables from curly maple for Susan and me.

The reader can use any of the four leg shapes shown on page 51 with equal success. A square tapered leg would also work well. The legs would be best tapered on the inside edges only. Construction details for the drawer can be found in the section on drawers and drawer construction starting on page 99. By turning the grain of the top at right angles to the drawing, a drop leaf could be added to each side of this table very successfully.

Choice of wood is not critical. The original has done about 150 years of faithful service in poplar. Good choices are cherry, walnut, maple or mahogany. The edge of the top of my table is square, which is faithful to the original. Other edge treatments could be used successfully, however. Nothing is hard and fast, just have fun!

# End Tables

**EARLY AMERICAN END TABLE**

**QUEEN ANNE END TABLE**

**SHAKER END TABLE**

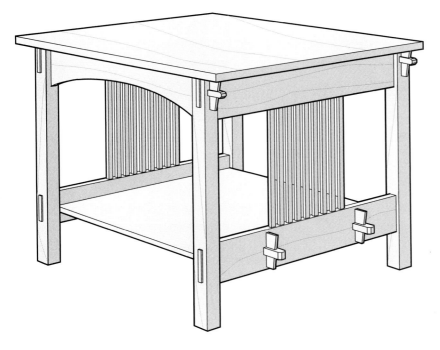

**CRAFTSMAN STYLE END TABLE**

# Early American End Table
## Dimensions

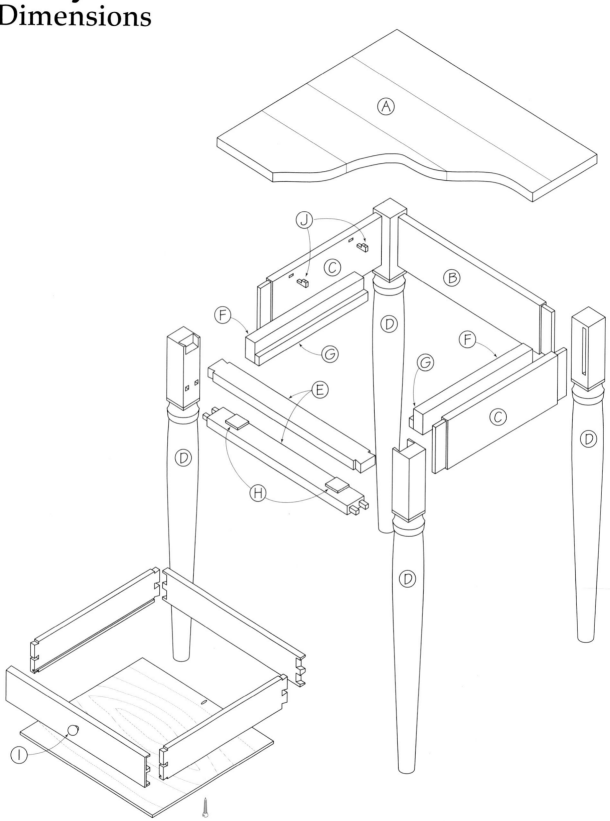

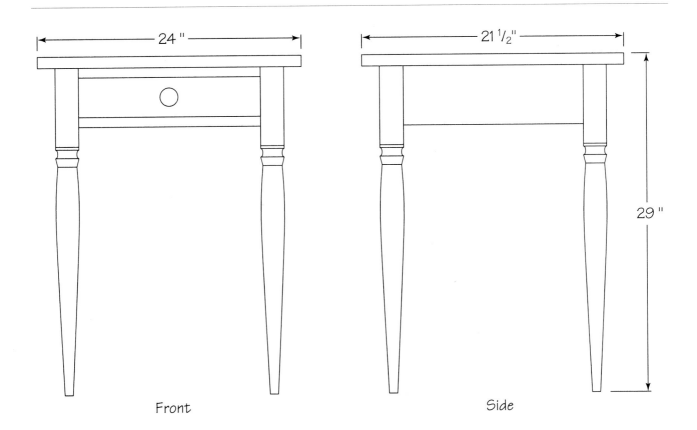

Front

Side

| CUTTING LIST—EARLY AMERICAN END TABLE | | |
|---|---|---|
| (a) Top | | ⅞" x 21 ½" x 24" |
| (b) Back Rail | | ¾" x 5" x 20" |
| (c) Side Rails | (2) | ¾" x 5" x 16" |
| (d) Legs | (4) | 2" x 2" x 23 ⅝" |
| (e) Front Rails | (2) | ⅞" x 2" x 20" |
| (f) Drawer Slides | (2) | 1 ¼" x 2" x 13" |
| (g) Drawer Slides | (2) | ½" x ½" x 13" |
| (h) Drawer Stops | (2) | ³⁄₁₆" x 1" x 1" |
| (i) Knob | | 2" x 2" x 4" |
| (j) Mortise Buttons | (4) | ¾" x 2" x 1" |

# Queen Anne End Table
## Dimensions

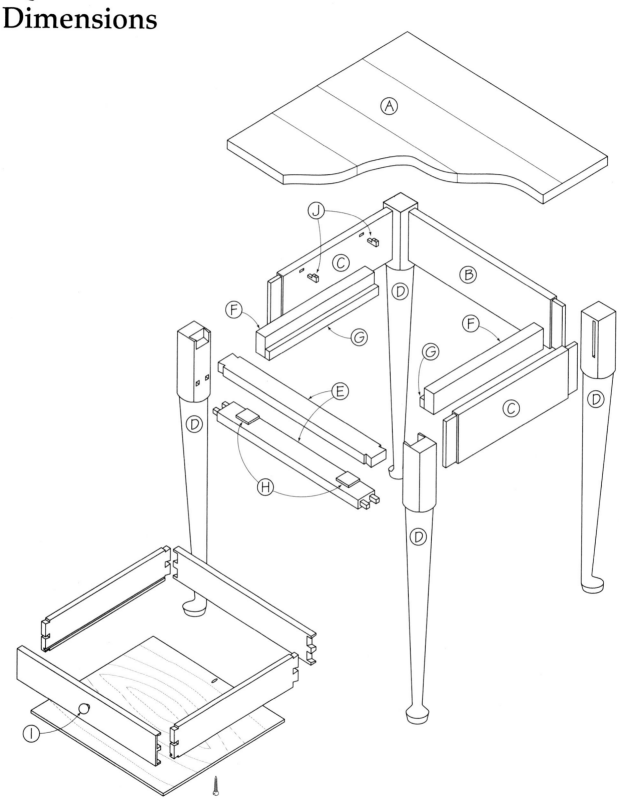

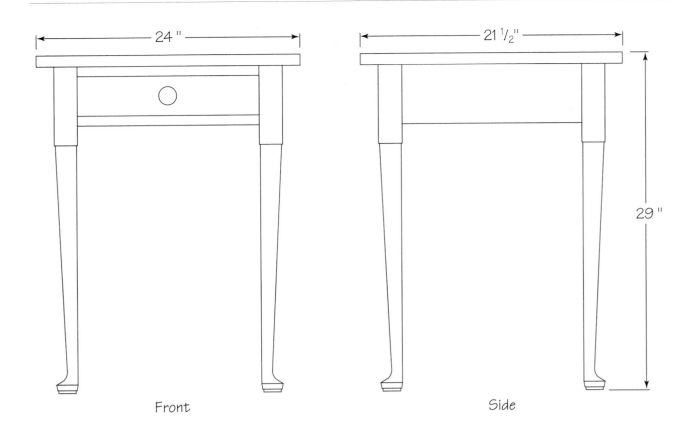

Front

Side

**CUTTING LIST—QUEEN ANNE END TABLE**

| | | |
|---|---|---|
| (a) Top | | 7/8" x 21 1/2" x 24" |
| (b) Back Rail | | 3/4" x 5" x 20" |
| (c) Side Rails | (2) | 3/4" x 5" x 16" |
| (d) Legs | (4) | 2" x 2" x 23 5/8" |
| (e) Front Rails | (2) | 7/8" x 2" x 20" |
| (f) Drawer Slides | (2) | 1 1/4" x 2" x 13" |
| (g) Drawer Slides | (2) | 1/2" x 1/2" x 13" |
| (h) Drawer Stops | (2) | 3/16" x 1" x 1" |
| (i) Knob | | 2" x 2" x 4" |
| (j) Mortise Buttons | (4) | 3/4" x 2" x 1" |

# Shaker End Table
## Dimensions

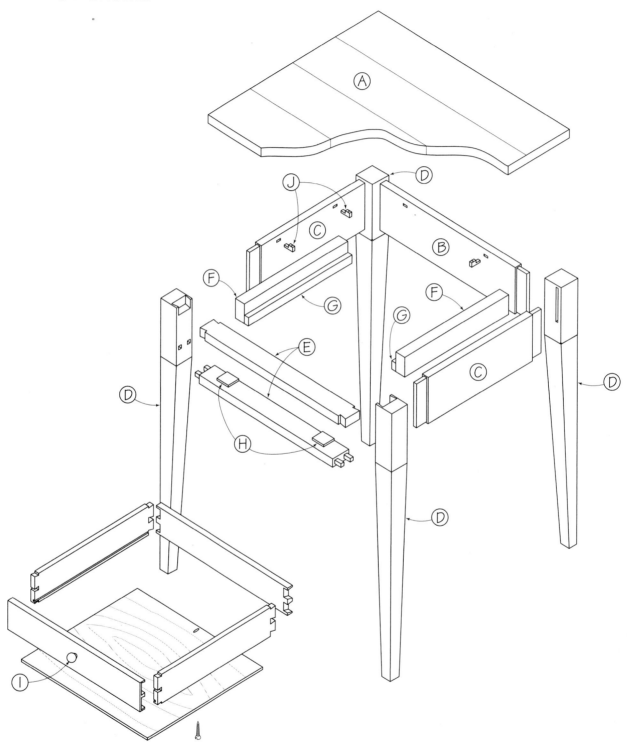

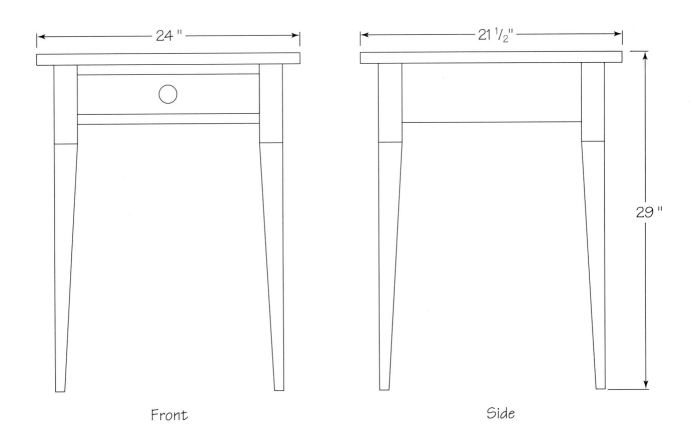

Front

Side

## CUTTING LIST—SHAKER END TABLE

| | | |
|---|---|---|
| (a) Top | | $\frac{7}{8}$" x 21 $\frac{1}{2}$" x 24" |
| (b) Back Rail | | $\frac{3}{4}$" x 5" x 20" |
| (c) Side Rails | (2) | $\frac{3}{4}$" x 5" x 16" |
| (d) Legs | (4) | 2" x 2" x 23 $\frac{5}{8}$" |
| (e) Front Rails | (2) | $\frac{7}{8}$" x 2" x 20" |
| (f) Drawer Slides | (2) | 1 $\frac{1}{4}$" x 2" x 13" |
| (g) Drawer Slides | (2) | $\frac{1}{2}$" x $\frac{1}{2}$" x 13" |
| (h) Drawer Stops | (2) | $\frac{3}{16}$" x 1" x 1" |
| (i) Knob | | 2" x 2" x 4" |
| (j) Mortise Buttons | (4) | $\frac{3}{4}$" x 2" x 1" |

# Craftsman End Table
## Dimensions

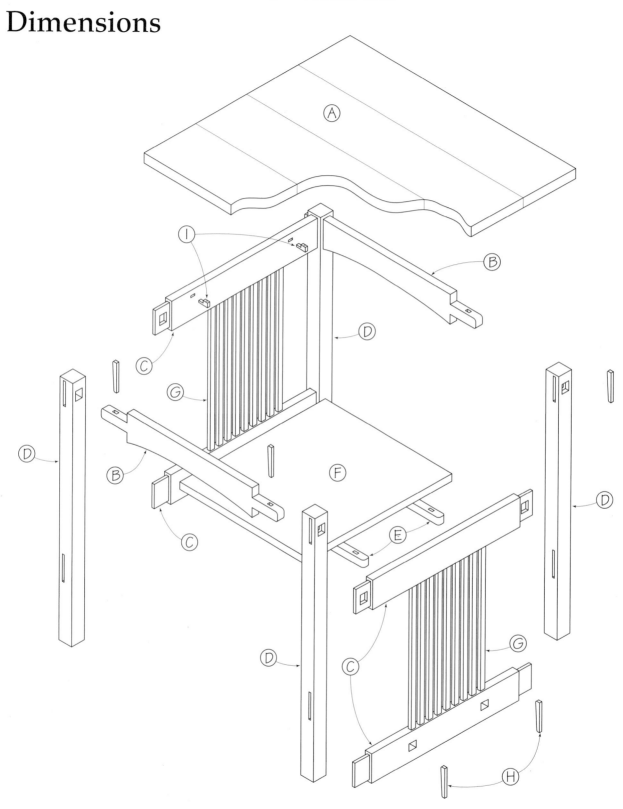

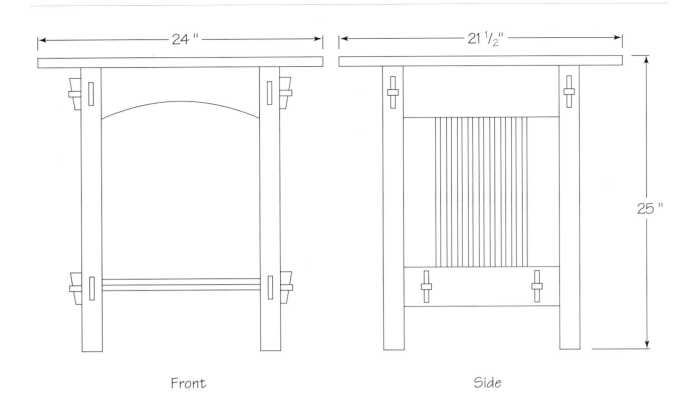

Front

Side

24"

21 1/2"

25"

**CUTTING LIST—CRAFTSMAN END TABLE**

| | | |
|---|---|---|
| (a) Top | | 7/8" x 21 1/2" x 24" |
| (b) Arched Front Rails | (2) | 3/4" X 3" X 21" |
| (c) End Rails | (4) | 3/4" X 3" X 20 1/4" |
| (d) Legs | (4) | 1 1/2" x 1 1/2" x 24" |
| (e) Shelf Support | (2) | 7/8" X 7/8" X 21" |
| (f) Shelf | | 7/8" X 15" X 21" |
| (g) Slats | (18) | 3/8" X 1/2" X 11 3/4" |
| (h) Wedges | (8) | 7/32" X 15/16" X 3 1/4" |
| (i) Mortise Buttons | (4) | 3/4" x 2" x 1" |

# CHAPTER TWO

# MAKING COFFEE TABLES

*This is a beautiful example of craftsman style oak furniture.*

Here you will find all of the dimensions and drawings to make four different coffee table designs. These tables are patterned after popular styles that can match your existing furniture. I built the craftsman style table, but the joinery is the same for the other table styles. Remember, you should feel free to adjust the height, length and width of any of these designs to suit your particular needs.

## CRAFTSMAN STYLE COFFEE TABLE

This table was a Christmas present to my son, Charlie, and his fiancée, Ana. Since Charlie's first job assignment takes him to Switzerland for five years, the table had to be easy to ship, easy to assemble, and easy to

knock down and be shipped again at the end of the assignment. It was made as a matching piece to a craftsman style futon bed I made him a few years ago.

Craftsman style is often called Mission Oak and the most famous practitioner of the craftsman style was Gustav Stickley. The Craftsman Movement was founded in England in the last quarter of the nineteenth century by the painter John Ruskin and the poet William Morris. Their "mission" was a rebellion against the excesses of the Victorian era and called for a return to hand craftsmanship. Craftsman style was a return to simple style and honest construction. A hallmark of the craftsman style was heavy use of mortise and tenon joinery (refreshing for anyone who has had to repair late Victorian furniture that is riddled with machine-made dowel joints). On tables, most tenons went through the mating leg and stood proud of the frame by about ⅛". The end of the tenon was beveled for decorative effect and commonly cross pinned. On both tables and case pieces, the tenon was often elegantly cross wedged. The wedged tenon lends itself well to knockdown construction, one of my design criteria. Although craftsman style furniture was executed in a variety of woods, it was most commonly done in oak. In fact, the man on the street thinks of no other wood but oak when the style is mentioned. The craftsman style led directly to Greene and Greene, Art Nouveau and Art Deco.

Of course, coffee tables were unknown in the craftsman period, but that should not keep us from trying to incorporate the spirit of craftsman design in our more modern incarnations. So as not to look to out of place, mine is scaled a little high for a coffee table, but this goes better with the futon bed, which is a bit high by seating standards when folded into a couch. Remember, you can easily modify this design by simply shortening the legs to bring the table top lower if you wish.

The table is a tour de force of mortise and tenon joints. Anyone constructing this table may want to think about investing in a hollow chisel mortising machine. In the ends of the table there are eight through mortises for the rails and thirty-six small mortises for the decorative vertical slats. There are eight more through mortises in the legs and rails for the side rails and eight corresponding cross mortises for the wedges. Altogether there are sixty mortises.

The finish was the same as Gustav Stickley used, namely fumed ammonia, shellac and wax. Stickley's original finish method was to construct a tent that his projects could fit inside, fill pans with ammonia and fume the project for several hours. (This is extremely dangerous and should be undertaken with the utmost safety and caution.) The ammonia fumes deepen the color of the wood and removes the red color of the oak. Shellac was then applied and the oak pores were brought out by rubbing with black tinted wax.

Rather than tent, I sponged on a 20 percent ammonia solution with a rag. It is imperative to wear a carbon vapor mask and have plenty of ventilation during this process. I used an air helmet which also covers my eyes. This gave the wood the rich brown color typical of Stickley pieces. I then padded a two pound cut of pale dewax shellac onto all surfaces. Once dry, I rubbed with black paste wax.

# Coffee Tables

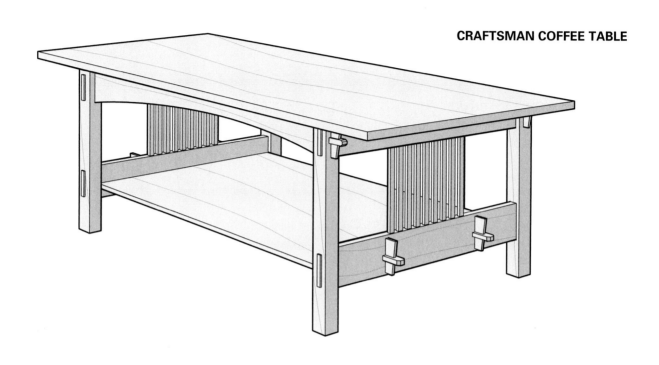

**CRAFTSMAN COFFEE TABLE**

**EARLY AMERICAN COFFEE TABLE**

**QUEEN ANNE COFFEE TABLE**

**SHAKER COFFEE TABLE**

# Craftsman Coffee Table
## Dimensions

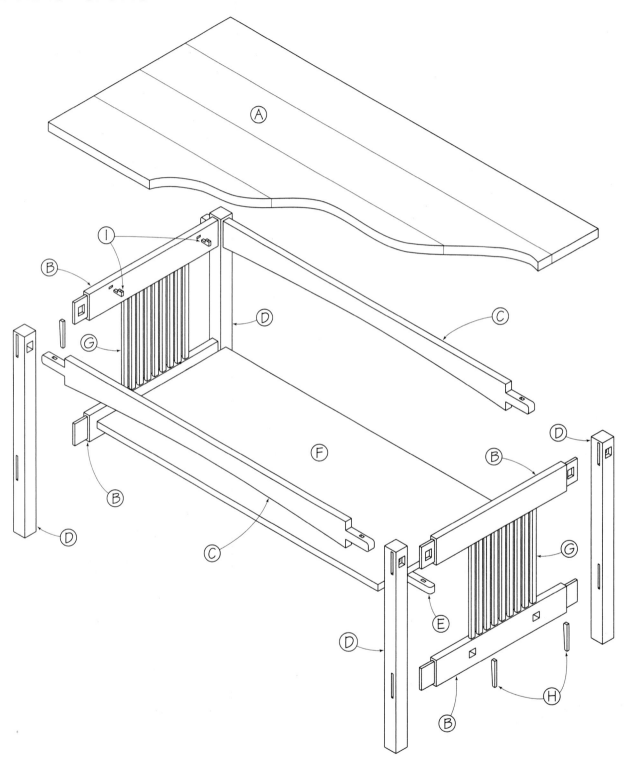

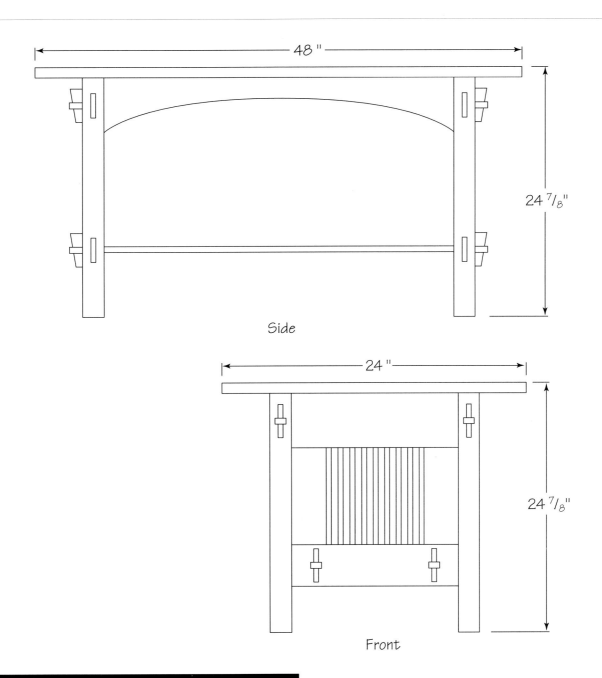

Side

Front

## CUTTING LIST—CRAFTSMAN COFFEE TABLE

| | | |
|---|---|---|
| (a) Top | | ⅞" x 24" x 48" |
| (b) End Rails | (4) | ¾" x 3" x 20 ¼" |
| (c) Arched Side Rails | (2) | ¾" x 3" x 43" |
| (d) Legs | (4) | 1 ½" x 1 ½" x 24" |
| (e) Bottom Side Rails | (2) | ⅞" x ⅞" x 43" |
| (f) Shelf | | ⅞" x 15" x 38" |
| (g) Slats | (18) | ⅜" x ½" x 11 ¾" |
| (h) Wedges | (8) | ⁷⁄₃₂" x ¹⁵⁄₁₆" x 3 ¼" |
| (i) Mortise Buttons | (4) | ¾" x 2" x 1" |

# Early American Coffee Table
## Dimensions

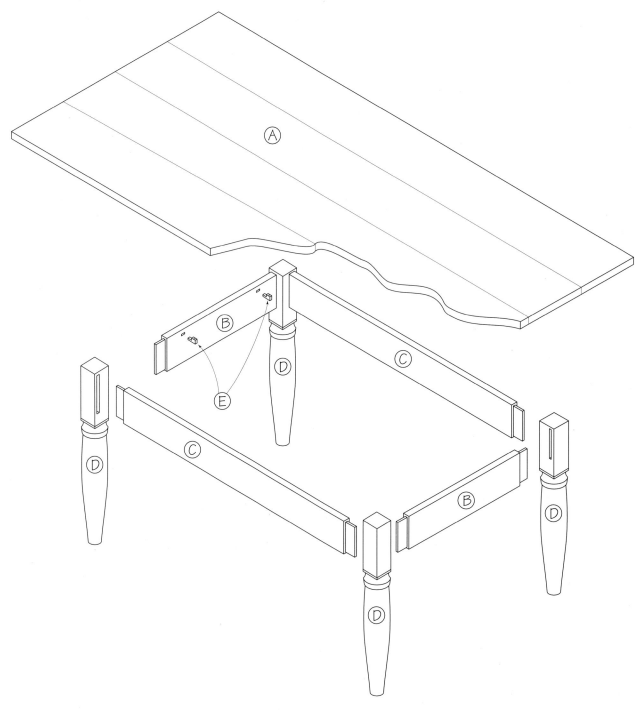

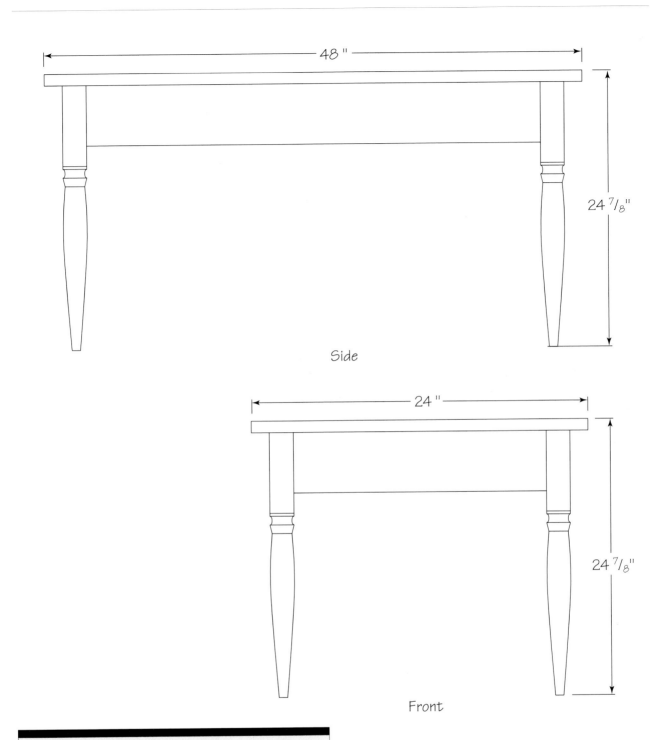

48 "

24 $^7/_8$"

Side

24 "

24 $^7/_8$"

Front

**CUTTING LIST—
EARLY AMERICAN COFFEE TABLE**

| | | |
|---|---|---|
| (a) Top | | $^7/_8$" x 24" x 48" |
| (b) End rails | (2) | $^3/_4$" x 3" x 20 $^1/_4$" |
| (c) Side rails | (2) | $^3/_4$" x 3" x 43" |
| (d) Legs | (4) | 2" x 2" x 24" |
| (e) Mortise buttons | (4) | $^3/_4$" x 2" x 1" |

# Queen Anne Coffee Table
## Dimensions

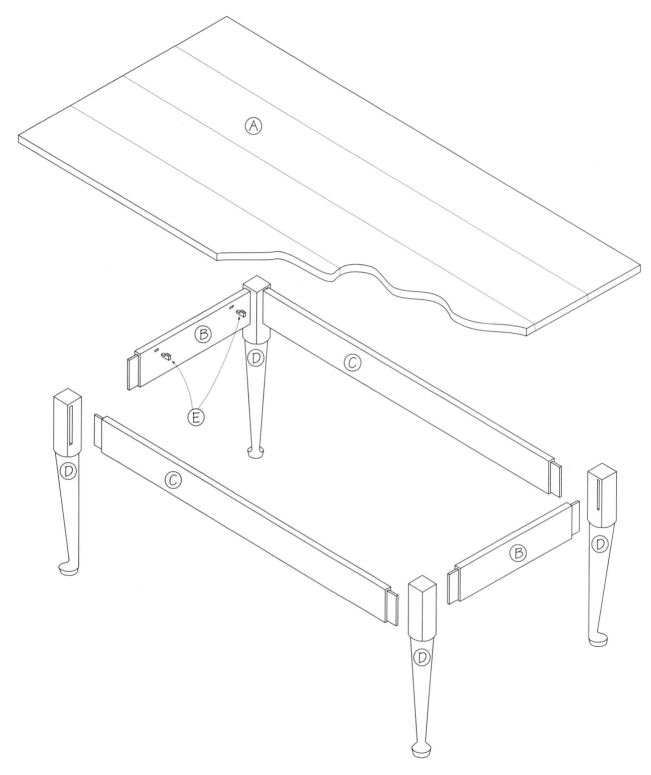

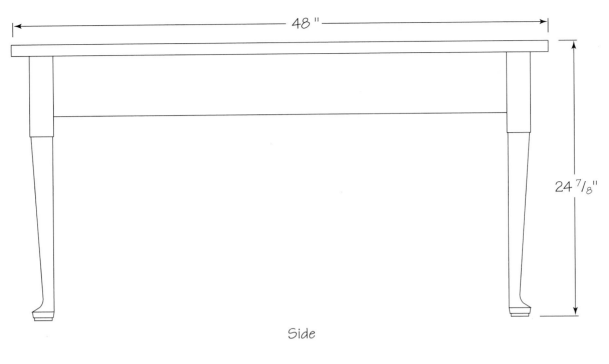

48 "

24 ⁷⁄₈"

Side

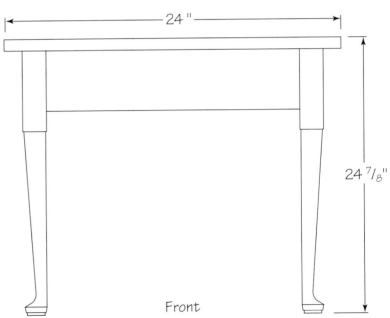

24 "

24 ⁷⁄₈"

Front

**CUTTING LIST—
QUEEN ANNE COFFEE TABLE**

| | | |
|---|---|---|
| (a) Top | | ⁷⁄₈" x 24" x 48" |
| (b) End rails | (2) | ¾" x 3" x 20 ¼" |
| (c) Side rails | (2) | ¾" x 3" x 43" |
| (d) Legs | (4) | 2" x 2" x 24" |
| (e) Mortise buttons | (8) | ¾" x 2" x 1" |

# Shaker Coffee Table
## Dimensions

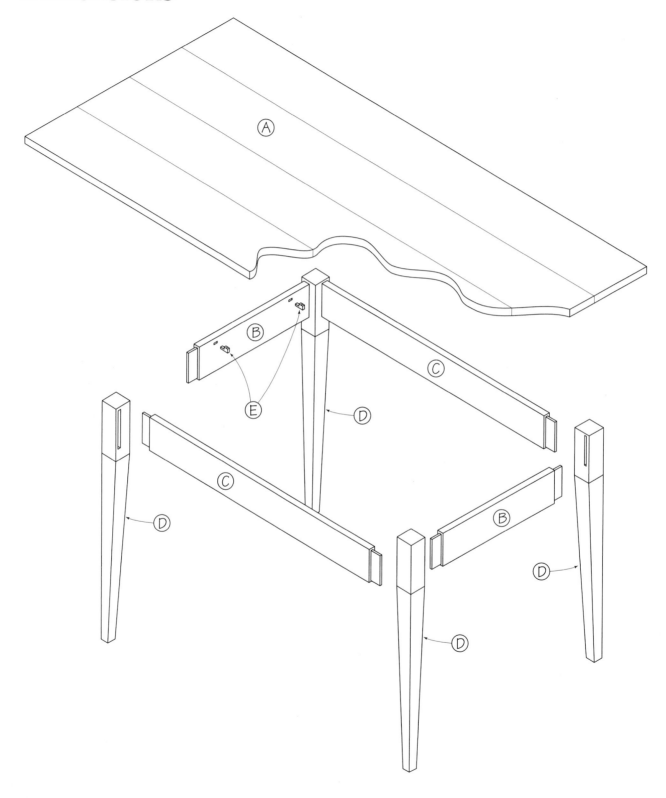

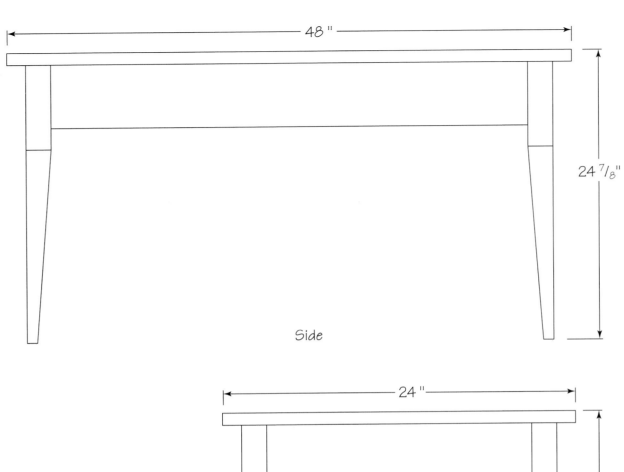

48 "

24 $^7/_8$"

Side

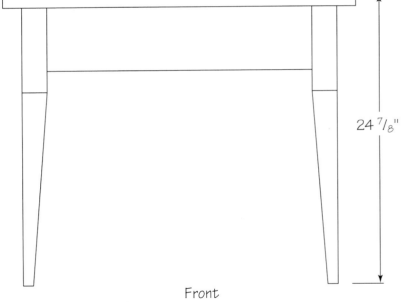

24 "

24 $^7/_8$"

Front

**CUTTING LIST—SHAKER COFFEE TABLE**

| | | |
|---|---|---|
| (a) Top | | $^7/_8$" x 24" x 48" |
| (b) End rails | (2) | $^3/_4$" x 3" x 20 $^1/_4$" |
| (c) Side rails | (2) | $^3/_4$" x 3" x 43" |
| (d) Legs | (4) | 2" x 2" x 24" |
| (e) Mortise buttons | (4) | $^3/_4$" x 2" x 1" |

# CHAPTER THREE

# MAKING DINING TABLES

*This smaller adaptation of a shaker dining table is made out of poplar and finished with milk paint.*

Dining tables serve as the most useful of all of the tables in this book. It is a great feeling to have built with your own hands the table that the family gathers around every night for dinner. Again, there are four styles presented here and the designs offered can be easily changed to incorporate the perfect size table for your needs. While not shown, you could easily adapt a silverware drawer into the end of your table or follow the instructions in chapter 7 for adding drop leaves. You can build the following designs as shown or change the size to suit your needs.

# SHAKER DINING TABLE

This table was built out of a need for a dining table on our screened in porch. The porch adjoins our kitchen through a large set of double doors. In the summer months, these doors are opened making what is essentially two rooms into one large area. Our kitchen table is the Shaker style dining table pictured on the cover of this book. My wife Susan and I wanted our porch table to mimic the style of the Shakers. Therefore, we decided to make a simple square table and to milk paint it, something the Shakers did frequently. This table would work equally well in a more formal setting if made from finer wood, such as cherry, maple or walnut, and given a clear finish.

I built the table out of yellow poplar, a wood we refer to as tulip because of the tree it is derived from. The large trunks of tulip trees (frequently 30" and more in diameter) can be found poking their branches up through the forest canopy all over Ohio. Often as not, the result is 30 to 60 feet of clear trunk without a branch. Yellow poplar is cheap, stable, most pleasant to work with and, best of all, takes paint well.

The 36" square shape of the top is designed for intimate dining for two to four people and cramped chaos for up to eight during summer picnics. The generous 5" overhang of the frame on all sides helps during these hectic times and allows easy traffic around the table if it is used for a buffet. People can walk right up to the edge without kicking the legs.

The design can easily be reconfigured for a variety of needs. The frame and top can be lengthened to make a more conventional rectangular shaped dining table. Cross bracing should be added, however, if the table is made longer than four feet. Because the table would be out in the elements I elected not to include a drawer, for it would only stick most of the time. For a rectangular shaped table designed for an inside setting, drawers on ends would add essential storage. The design would also adapt well to a drop leaf scheme. The main top has a drawer at each side and will accommodate two diners with ease. The two drop leaves can be raised for commodious accommodations for four or even six with some cramping. A square tapered leg, or any of the turned legs, can be substituted as suits your personal taste.

# Dining Tables

**SHAKER DINING TABLE**

**EARLY AMERICAN DINING TABLE**

**CRAFTSMAN DINING TABLE**

**QUEEN ANNE DINING TABLE**

# Shaker Dining Table
## Dimensions

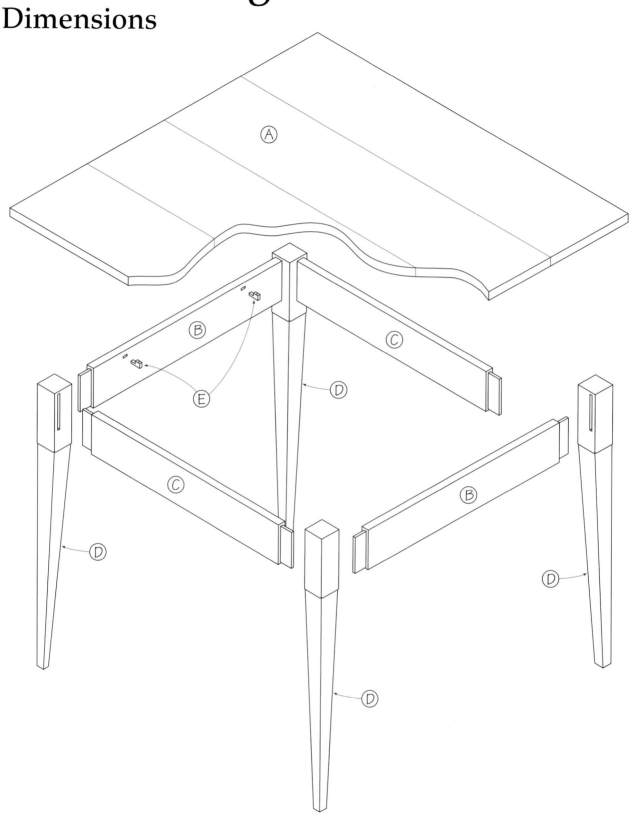

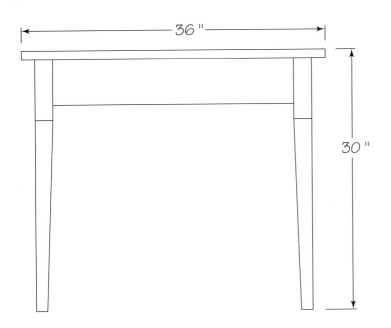

Front

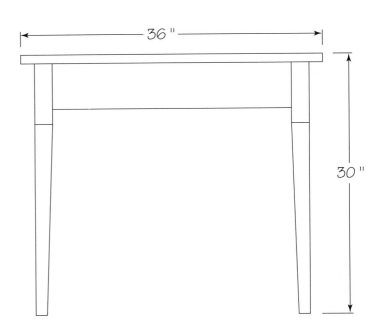

Side

**CUTTING LIST—SHAKER DINING TABLE**

| | | |
|---|---|---|
| (a) Top | | ⅞" x 36" x 36" |
| (b) End Rails | (2) | ¾" x 4" x 25" |
| (c) Side Rails | (2) | ¾" x 4" x 25" |
| (d) Legs | (4) | 2" x 2" x 29 ¼" |
| (e) Mortise Buttons | (4) | ¾" x 2" x 1" |

# Early American Dining Table
## Dimensions

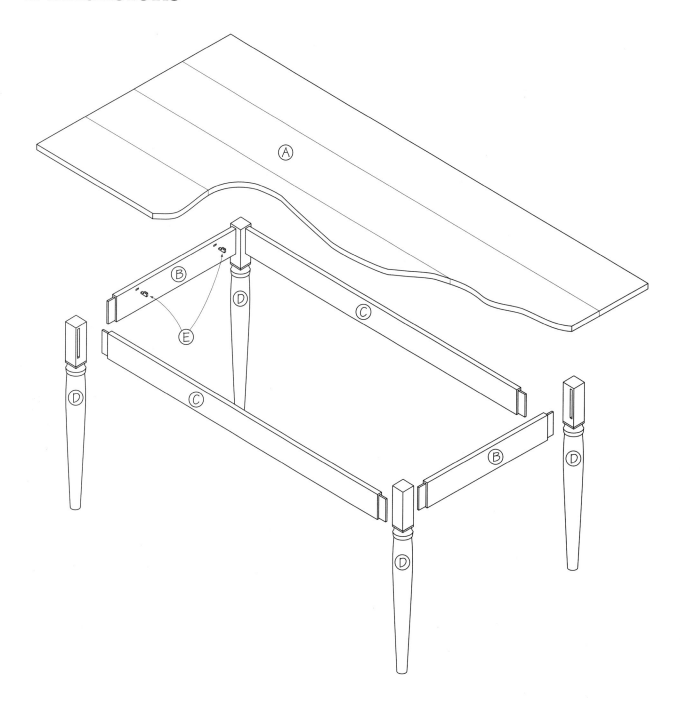

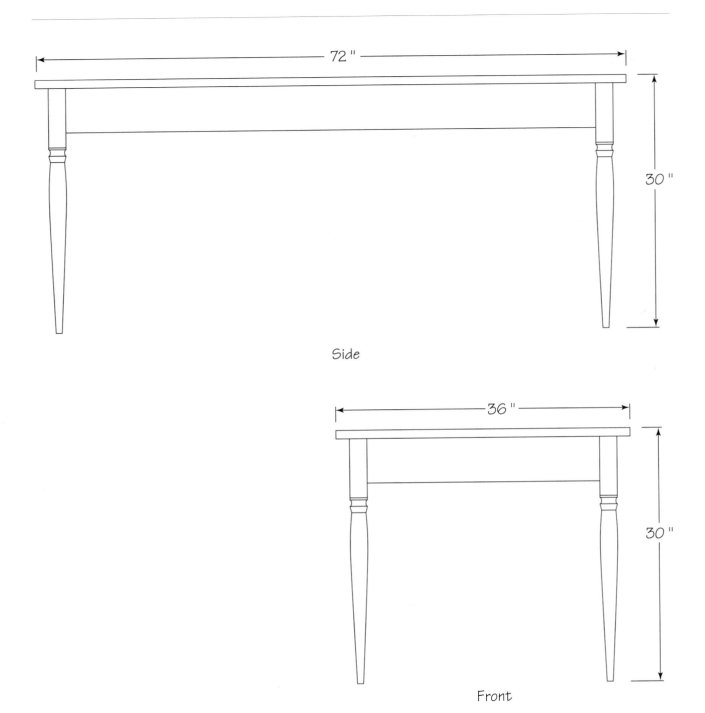

Side

Front

**CUTTING LIST
—EARLY AMERICAN DINING TABLE**

| | | |
|---|---|---|
| (a) Top | | $\frac{7}{8}$" x 36" x 72" |
| (b) End Rails | (2) | $\frac{3}{4}$" x 4" x 25" |
| (c) Side Rails | (2) | $\frac{3}{4}$" x 4" x 65" |
| (d) Legs | (4) | 2" x 2" x 29 $\frac{1}{4}$" |
| (e) Mortise Buttons | (4) | $\frac{3}{4}$" x 2" x 1" |

# Craftsman Dining Table
## Dimensions

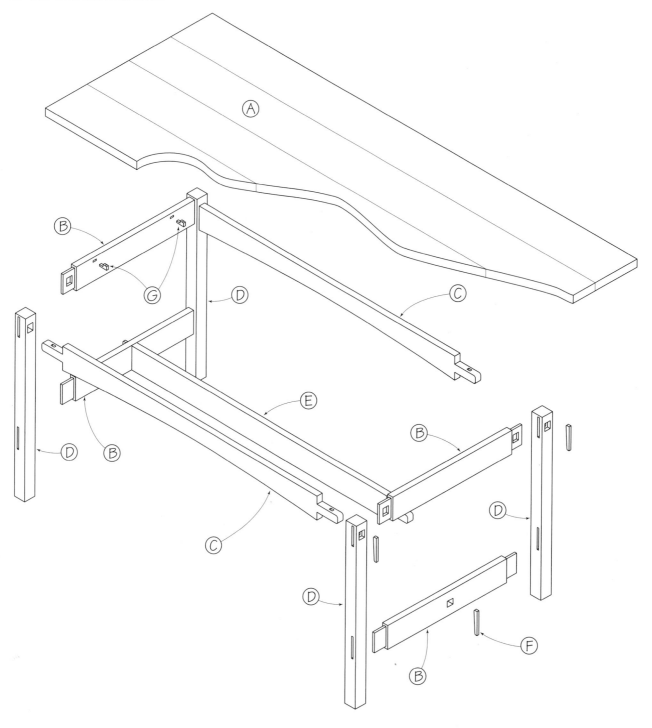

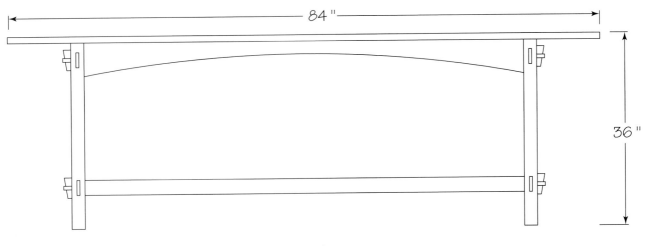

Side

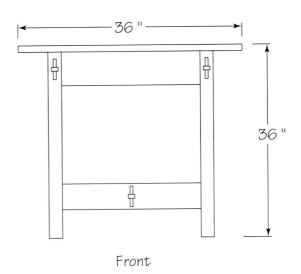

Front

**CUTTING LIST—CRAFTSMAN DINING TABLE**

| | | |
|---|---|---|
| (a) Top | | 1" X 36" X 84" |
| (b) End rails | (4) | ¾" X 3 ¾" X 25" |
| (c) Arched side rails | (2) | ¾" X 3 ¾" X 53" |
| (d) Legs | (4) | 1 ⅞" X 1 ⅞" X 30" |
| (e) Center stretcher | | ¾" X 3 ¾" X 72 ½" |
| (f) Wedges | (6) | ⁷⁄₃₂" X ¹⁵⁄₁₆" X 3 ¼" |
| (g) Mortise buttons | (6) | ¾" X 1" X 2" |

# Queen Anne Dining Table
## Dimensions

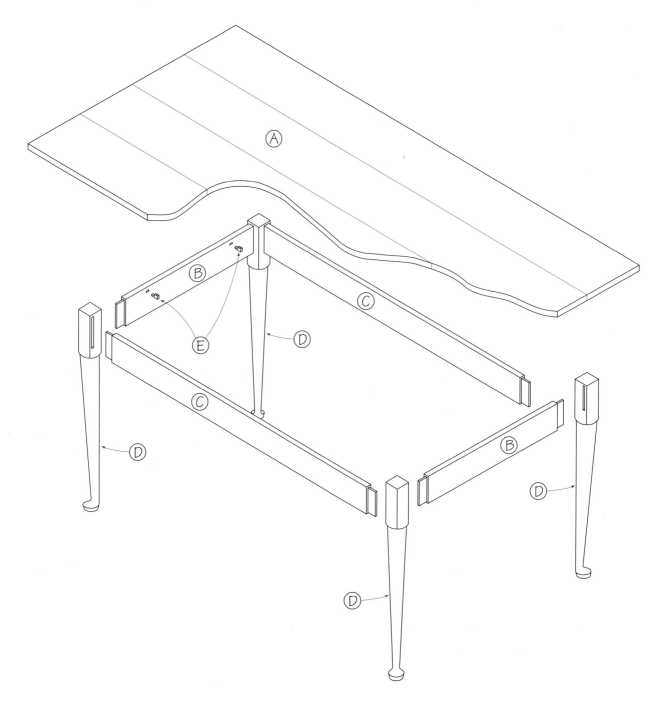

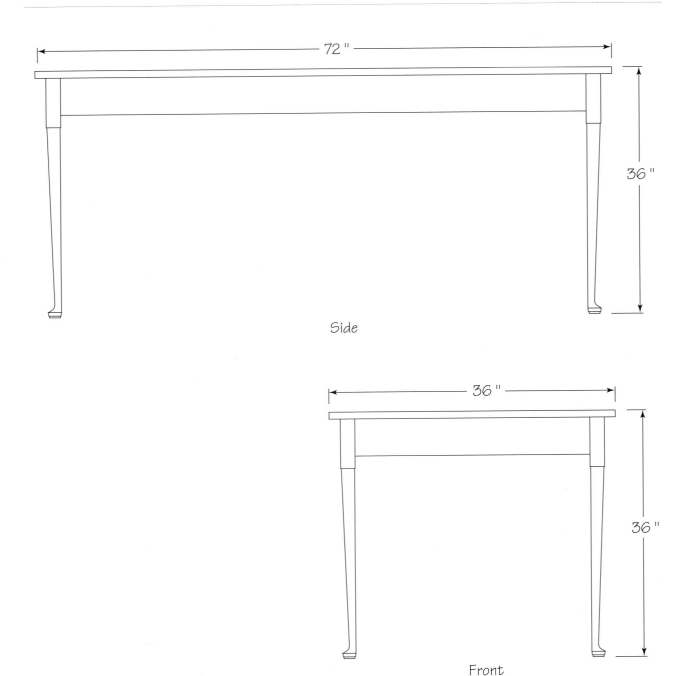

72 "

36 "

Side

36 "

36 "

Front

**CUTTING LIST—QUEEN ANNE DINING TABLE**

| | | |
|---|---|---|
| (a) Top | | ⅞" x 36" x 72" |
| (b) End rails | (2) | ¾" x 4" x 25" |
| (c) Side rails | (2) | ¾" x 4" x 65" |
| (d) Legs | (4) | 2" x 2" x 29 ¼" |
| (e) Mortise buttons | (10) | ¾" x 2" x 1" |

# PART TWO

# TECHNIQUES

# MAKING TABLE LEGS

To quote an old cliché, "he doesn't have a leg to stand on," a position we definitely don't want to be in as furniture makers. So it seems to me that legs are the most basic components in a table, and the thing I generally go about making first. Legs can be of simple square construction, turned on a lathe, or even sculpted and carved.

## BUYING LUMBER

The first task in building any leg is to mill square billets of the proper size and length. I generally try to obtain solid material for my legs; however, gluing up is also a viable option. If the glue joint is done well (both surfaces are jointed), the resulting leg can actually be stronger than a solid one. Theory says to reverse the grains from each other so that stress will be equalized.

Hardwood lumber is usually sold rough-sawn, although increasingly

suppliers are offering custom milling services. Rough-sawn wood is sold by the quarters of a inch with four quarter (it is referred to in just this way but written 4/4) being the thinnest routinely available size. The rough-sawn board will not be 1" thick, however, but rather at least 1 ⅛" thick. The extra gives allowances for planing, but one can seldom obtain 1" from 4/4 rough-sawn stock. If you are lucky, you will get ¹⁵⁄₁₆", with ⅞" being more likely. Most any dealer stocks 4/4 and 8/4 material with better dealers also offering 5/4, 6/4, and thicker material up to 16/4. It is best to purchase material at least ¼" thicker than you need for the leg. While most commercial furniture factories only use select lumber that is entirely free of knots and defects, the small production builder is often better to select a lower grade of material (down to and including #2 common). While this material will have knots, you can work around them. The grain in such wood will be much more interest-

ing. When working with hardwoods, it is best to figure one-third waste; so buy one third more material than you need.

## MILLING ROUGH STOCK

Once the rough material is in hand, the power jointer, table saw and thickness planer are best employed to arrive at square billets of the proper size and length. Square a face and an edge on the jointer, rip oversize squares on the table saw, and mill to exact size with the thickness planer. The following sections show how the milling and tapering of the leg is done. The best solution for those lacking these tools is to have your lumber supplier do the milling for you. Dimensioned lumber is referred to by its actual size (e.g., ¾", 1⅞", etc.). Finding dealers that stock dimensioned material other than ¾" (often ¹³⁄₁₆") or 1⅞" is difficult and expensive.

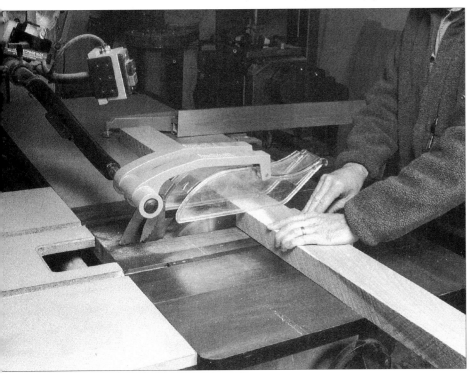

**STEP 1**

## MAKING SQUARE LEGS

**STEP 1**

# Preparing Rough Stock

Start by cutting rough-sawn planks to just a bit longer than the leg you plan to make. If you are to employ mortise and tenon construction, you will need to add 1" to the leg length. The extra inch at the top of the leg helps to prevent it from splitting during mortising and is cut off before assembly. Always discard 2" to 4" from the end of the plank, for there is invariably checking in this area from the drying process that could affect the final leg.

**STEP 2**

**STEP 2**

# Joint One Edge 90° to Another

True one face and an edge on the jointer. Lacking a jointer you can use a jack plane for this job.

# Rip Leg Blanks

Rip slightly oversize (1/32" to 1/16")
squares on the table saw. Re-joint
each sawn edge on the jointer
before ripping the next square, so as
to always have a jointed true face
and true edge.

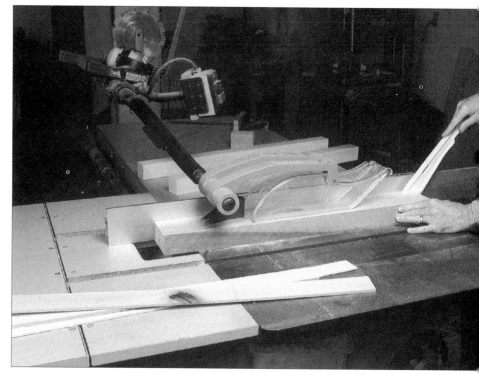

**STEP 3**

# Bring to Finish Size

Use the thickness planer to bring
the billet to final size. Always place
the joined face on the bed of the
planer so that material is only
removed from the sawn face.

**STEP 4**

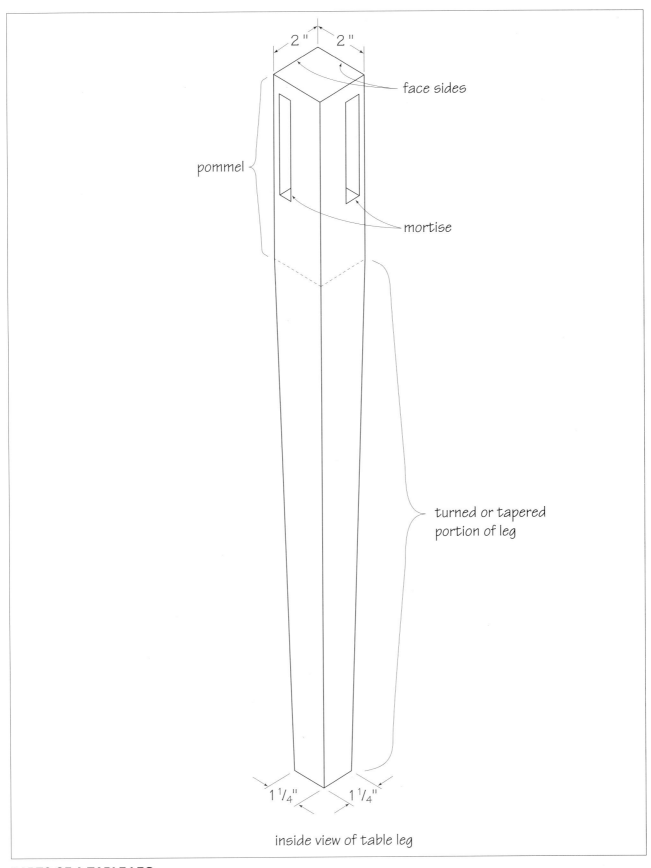

2 " 2 "

face sides

pommel

mortise

turned or tapered
portion of leg

1 1/4" 1 1/4"

inside view of table leg

## PARTS OF A TABLE LEG

*No matter what the method of construction, the vocabulary is the same, and we will use these terms throughout the book.*

# MAKING A TAPERED LEG

After the square leg, the simplest leg to build is a tapered square leg. It takes the minimum of equipment and can even be made entirely with hand tools. A slight taper starting below the pommel adds a sophistication to an otherwise straight leg. More sophisticated forms are tapered on more than two sides below the pommel.

Tapering adds a lighter, more refined look to a leg and a lightness to the design. It is common to many furniture styles. Most legs are only tapered on the inside edges and such tapers are easily done on the table saw. If your design requires tapering from all four sides, a jointer or a hand plane is better employed.

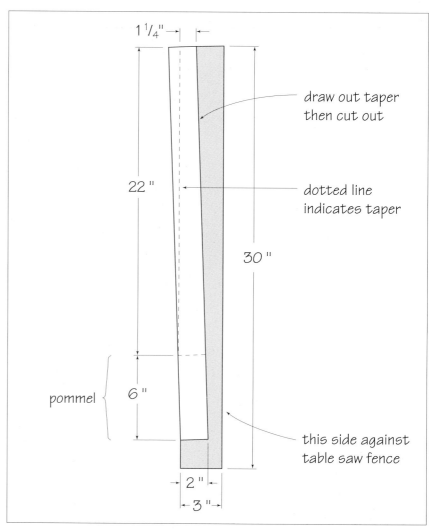

draw out taper then cut out

dotted line indicates taper

this side against table saw fence

$1\frac{1}{4}$"

22 "

30 "

pommel

6 "

2 "

3 "

**SHOP-MADE TABLE SAW TAPERING JIG**

## MAKING TAPERED LEGS ON THE JOINTER

### STEP 1

## Mark the Blank

Mark out the pommel and the size of the square at the bottom that you plan to taper to. This will tell you the taper.

**STEP 1**

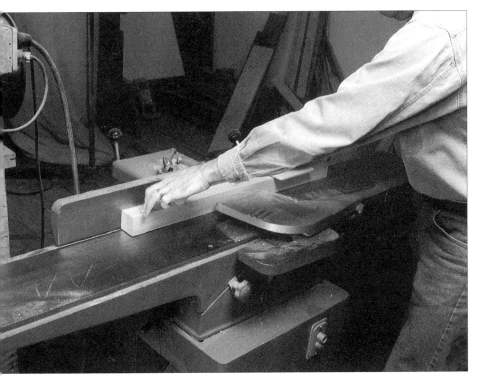

**STEP 2**

## Make the First Cut

Place the middle of the taper over the knives and make the first cut. The guard must be eased out of the way, and great care should be exercised when setting the work down on the tables. Be sure to use push sticks/blocks to advance the work. It is best to take light passes in the neighborhood of ¹⁄₁₆" to ⅛". Do each of the legs in turn.

**STEP 3**

**STEP 3**

## Finish the Blanks

Repeat the above process with each leg in turn as many times as necessary to arrive at the correct taper. Each successive pass should be closer to the pommel with the final being at the start of the taper. Check with the marks for the pommel and the bottom square frequently.

## MAKING TAPERED LEGS WITH A HAND PLANE

For just four legs, I think a hand plane offers the best option. There is no setup, the possibility of a mistake is negligible, and the finish is superlative. For a production run of legs, I would employ a table saw or a jointer, but I would still use a plane for final smoothing because sanding is minimized. I start with a jack plane (O5) and make the final passes with the longer jointer plane (O7 or O8).

### STEP 1
## Mark the Blank

Mark out the pommel and the square that you plan to taper to at the bottom of the leg. This will tell you the taper. Dog the leg down in the bench and plane toward the foot of the leg. Plane more at the foot at first and move progressively farther back with each pass.

### STEP 2
## Using the Jointer Plane

Make final passes with the jointer plane. It's longer body will clean up any marks left by the jack plane.

**STEP 1**

**STEP 2**

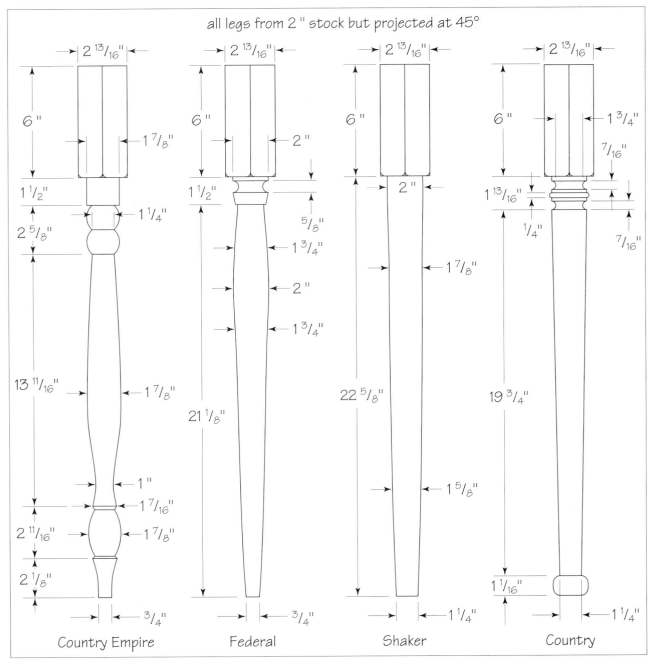

**TURNED LEG SHAPES**

# MAKING TURNED LEGS

Turning is my preferred method of leg construction. This is not to say that every leg must be turned, for this would limit design and become boring if done to excess. Turning, however, adds pizzazz and interest to design and is essential to many Victorian styles of furniture. Actually turning four legs is quite simple and makes a fun sub-project to the building of a table.

Any turned leg must start with a square billet and the same process previously described in "Milling Rough Stock" on page 44. The main problems in turning any leg are actual turning techniques and duplicating parts.

Turned legs take two forms, simple turned and cabriole-type legs that must be offset during the turning process. Either is really quite simple to turn, and the following examples should give you all of the information necessary to tackle turned legs.

## DUPLICATING TURNED LEG SHAPES

Duplication of parts is really quite easy. One hang-up of late-twentieth-century man is that duplicate connotes plus or minus .0005". For woodturnings, plus or minus 1/16" is more in order. The unwritten assignment to the viewer of your four table legs is "make these darn things look alike." The human eye has such a passion for symmetry that it will make them look alike—even if they are not. Therefore we only have to turn the same theme from leg to leg. If you get the major diameter (the thickest part of the turning) and the minor diameter (the smallest part of the turning) the same and place all of the elements of the turning at the same height from the floor, the human eye will do the rest. Think of yourself as a magician rather than a turner, you are fooling the audience.

**STEP 1**

## STEP 1
# Turn Billets Round

Start with carefully milled billets that are 1/16" oversize and the exact center carefully marked out. By just turning these billets round you will arrive at the correct major diameter for your leg. You do not need calipers to measure this major diameter for careful centering; just turning it round will give it.

**STEP 2**

## STEP 2
# Obtain Desired Diameter

Calipers are invaluable in sizing intermediate and minor diameters. Size the area using the cutoff tool and the caliper as a team to obtain the desired diameter.

**STEP 3**

## Layout Offset Distances

Dividers are super for laying offset distances such as the height of a foot.

**STEP 4**

## Using Pattern Sticks

Pattern sticks are an easy way to ensure that each element is placed at the right height from the floor, and they provide a visual reference for shaping each leg the same. They may be stored as a reference source, should you ever want to make another table with the same leg design.

# A Shop-Made Steady Rest

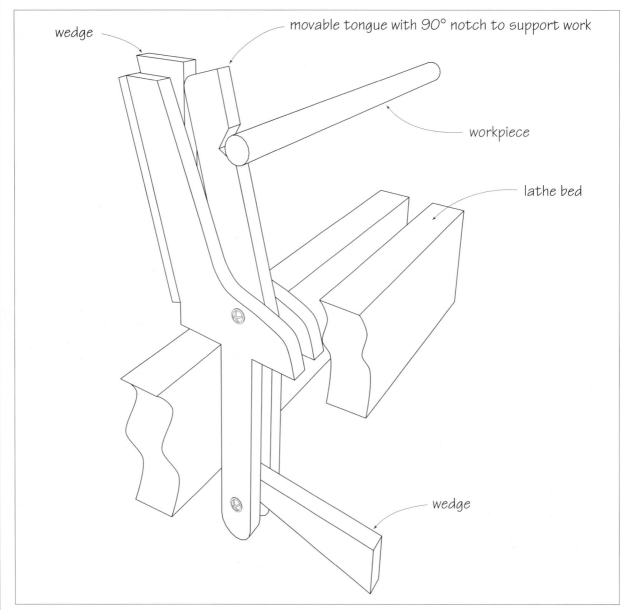

wedge

movable tongue with 90° notch to support work

workpiece

lathe bed

wedge

**STEADY REST**

A steady rest can be of great help in turning longer legs, for it will eliminate the harmonic chatter that results when long, thin turnings vibrate against the tool. A steady rest contacts the turning just off of center and dampens the vibration with the result that the turning is sure and chatter free. The one in use here is shop built. A steady rest is worth considering on any turning 15" or longer. The exact length at which to use a steady rest is, of course, dictated by the diameter of the turning. The thinner the turning, the shorter the length that you will have to employ the steady rest.

**STEP 5**

# Set Up a Steady Rest

Mount the steady rest slightly off center. This breaks up the two resulting halves of the turning into uneven frequencies.

**STEP 6**

# Turn Stock Round

Turn the piece round at the point under the rest, but leave it just a bit proud of the actual diameter you will actually want. Calipers are good for this. Use a ½" spindle gouge for this task, for it will bring the piece perfectly round.

# Wax Steady Rest Contact Points

Apply wax as a lubricant to the area you have brought round that contacts the steady rest. Bring the steady rest into play and turn normally. A bit of burning is normal at times.

**STEP 7**

# Finishing Up

When the turning is finished, remove the steady rest and turn and finish the area under it.

**STEP 8**

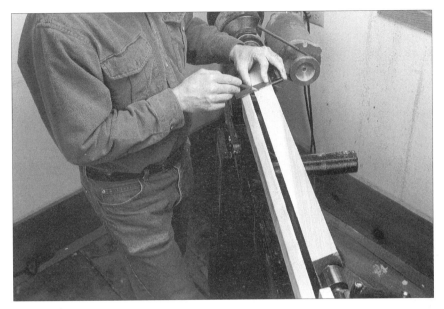

**STEP 1**

# LEGS TURNED ON ONE AXIS

Most table legs are turned on one axis—the billet is chucked on center, and the piece is turned. This is what we normally think of as a turned leg. It can range from extremely simple (as in the case of the following Shaker leg) to very ornate and complicated (as would be the case with Empire and Victorian designs).

## TURNING A SIMPLE SHAKER LEG

**STEP 1**

## Mark Out The Billet

Start with a perfectly square billet chucked on center. Mark out the terminus of the pommel.

**STEP 2**

## Work the Pommel From Square to Round

Use a gouge to make the transition from the square pommel area to the round leg itself.

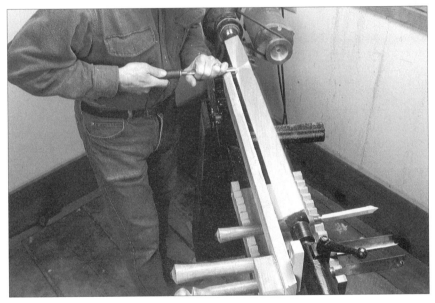

**STEP 2**

## STEP 3

# Bring to a Constant Diameter

Use a roughing gouge to bring the leg just round and to a constant diameter.

**STEP 3**

## STEP 4

# Size the Foot Diameter

Use calipers and a cutoff tool to size the foot diameter.

## STEP 5

# Finish the Leg

Use the roughing gouge and a skew to finalize the taper. Sand and finish the leg to taste.

**STEP 4**

**58** TABLES YOU CAN CUSTOMIZE

# MAKING TURNED CABRIOLE LEGS

Cabriole legs date back to Egyptian times, but they are most often associated with Queen Anne style furniture. True cabriole legs are sweeping, graceful arches that often resemble an animal's foot. They are cut to rough form on a band saw then sculpted to final shape with drawknives, spokeshaves, rasps, files and sandpaper. Such legs are often further embellished with carving such as shell patterns at the top of the leg or a clawed animal foot holding a ball at the bottom. Queen Anne is one of the most popular styles in America, and numerous reproductions have been made from the early nineteenth century right up to the present. One only needs to walk into any furniture store to realize that the styles still captivates. Most production furniture, however, has legs that are simple in form compared to the originals.

Cabriole legs can also be turned. Such legs were often used in the Queen Anne period on country pieces and chairs. Turned cabriole legs were also used as the back legs of finer pieces when the customer wanted to save money or when the piece had to go against a wall. Turned legs do not flare like sculpted ones do; in fact, they actually taper inward. Still, they give the look and feel of Queen Anne without anywhere near the work of the sculpted variety. Since most commercial Queen Anne legs are simple in nature (often machine turned), few people will have any objection to turned legs these days.

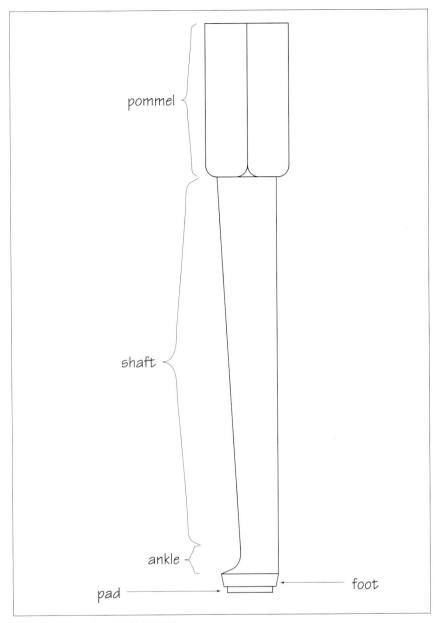

**PARTS OF A CABRIOLE LEG**
*Pommel, shaft, ankle, foot and pad.*

Cabriole legs are turned by chucking the work on center and turning the area below the pommel just round. The pad and the foot are then laid out and turned. The billet is now offset to turn the taper below the pommel, the ankle and the top of the foot. Both ends of the billet are offset in opposite directions and the amount of the offset has to be precisely figured to achieve the correct taper and ankle diameter. See the sidebar on page 60 on how to figure the offsets. The following section on turning a cabriole leg should give sufficient information to turn them yourself.

# Figuring the Offsets for a Turned Cabriole Leg

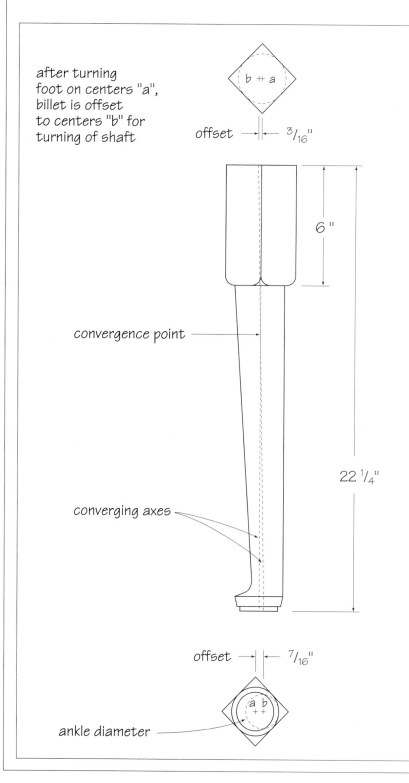

after turning
foot on centers "a",
billet is offset
to centers "b" for
turning of shaft

$b + a$

offset → ← $^3/_{16}$"

6"

convergence point

22 $^1/_4$"

converging axes

offset → ← $^7/_{16}$"

$a$ $b$

ankle diameter

The easiest way to figure the offsets is to draw out the desired leg either full-size or to scale. If to scale, you will need at least half-scale to get accurate measurements. The pommel length and the ankle diameter really determine the offset. Simply extend the center point of the ankle to the bottom of the foot and this is the offset at that end of the billet. Now extend a line from this new offset center point to the original centerline just under the pommel. This is the point where you want the old and new axes to converge so as to have a continuous taper from the pommel to the ankle. Now extend the line to the top of the turning, and you have the top offset point which is always less than the bottom offset.

**STEP 1**

### STEP 1

# Mark Out the Billet

Start by marking out the centers and the offset points at both ends. For this leg the offset at the foot is $\frac{7}{16}$", and at the top it is $\frac{5}{32}$".

**STEP 2**

### STEP 2

# Turn the Leg Round

Make the transition from square to round at the base of the pommel and turn the rest of the leg just round.

## TURNING A
## CABRIOLE LEG

STEP 3

# Begin the Foot
# Turning

Lay out the pad, then the foot, and
turn the pad and bottom half of the
foot.

**STEP 3**

STEP 4

# Change Center
# Points

Now offset the turning to the new
center points.

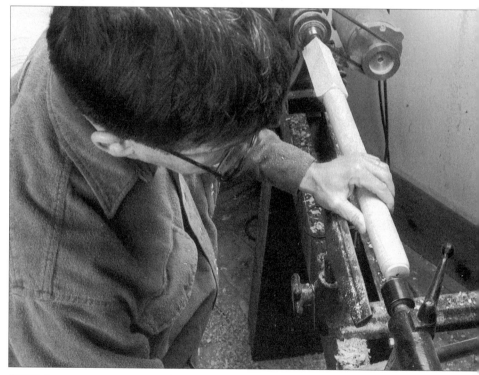

**STEP 4**

**STEP 5**

# Turn the Rest Of the Leg

Turn the shaft, ankle, and the top of the foot.

**STEP 6**

# Finish the Leg

Sand and finish to taste.

## USING PRE MADE CABRIOLE LEGS

It is also possible to purchase cabriole legs ready-made. This may be a good option for those in a hurry or lacking a lathe or the tools for sculpting a true cabriole leg. If you want to try sculpting a true leg yourself, there are ample texts on the subject. *Display Cabinets You Can Customize* by Jeff Greef, published by Betterway Books, has a step by step section on sculpting cabriole legs. For sources of ready-made legs, see Sources of Supply on page 113.

# CHAPTER FIVE

# MAKING TABLE APRONS

Aprons are the horizontal members that in conjunction with the four legs form the frame to support the top. They are the basis of frame construction and are usually simple, rectangular sections of wood that anchor the legs and support the top. Sometimes they are decorative in their own right with patterns sawn in the bottom edge.

## APRON JOINERY OPTIONS

The aprons can be attached to the leg by various methods—mortise and tenon joinery being the traditional method. Biscuit joinery or

dowel pins may be substituted for mortise and tenon joinery, but strength suffers. Finally, there is a variety of hardware available today to attach the leg to the apron. We shall now look at all of these frame construction methods.

## MORTISE AND TENON JOINERY

Mortise and tenon joinery is the traditional method of frame construction, and even today it is the most substantial. It is my preferred method. There are other methods that can be employed by woodworkers. For portability, many tables

are constructed using knockdown construction. Special hardware for this purpose is discussed on page 88.

This variation of the traditional mortise and tenon employs a haunched tenon below and a so called "modern" tenon on page 65; however, as we will learn, there is nothing modern about it. Cutting a haunched tenon is vastly more work than the modern tenon, but this style is taught in many traditional hand- tool joinery texts and woodworking schools. The reason for the haunch is obscure, and I have heard a variety of reasons for its presence. The only argument that holds water is that the additional height provided by the haunch gives additional anti-racking strength to the table without making the tenon itself

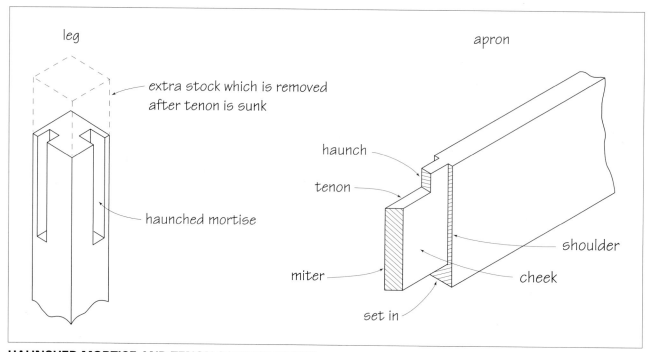

**HAUNCHED MORTISE AND TENON CONSTRUCTION**

overly wide. As you will see in the sidebar "Wood Movement" on page 67, a tenon should not be overly wide, for the chance of a glue-joint failure becomes proportionally greater as the tenon gets wider. Under this theory, glue should not be applied to the haunch area, only to the main tenon. The main use of haunched tenons is in building mortise and tenon panel doors with hand tools. The groove for the panel can be plowed the length of the rail, and the haunch on the rail fills the groove at the top and bottom of the panel. In reality the modern tenon is what most workers use, and examination of antique tables shows that the haunched tenon was seldom used by our forefathers. Let us examine the modern joint in detail.

## MAKING A MORTISE AND TENON JOINT

Whether you are cutting mortise and tenons by hand or by machine, the mortise is chopped first. This is because the width of the mortise is dependent on the width of the hand mortising chisel, machine hollow mortising chisel or router bit. The tenon must be made to fit the mortise. The two parts should slide together easily dry but with no play side to side. (In a proper fit, the glue will cause sufficient swelling for the two pieces to be difficult to disassemble if this should become necessary before the glue sets. This is why glue ups should be well thought out.) There must be some play in height (usually about ¹⁄₁₆" to ⅛"), for the tenon will change in height with changes in humidity while the height of the mortise will not. (See "Wood Movement" on page 67.) The only place the glue will do any good is on the cheeks of the tenon, for the top and bottom of the mortise are end grain. Whether mortising by hand or machine, it is common to leave about 1" extra at the top of the leg which is removed as waste once the mortises are chopped. This extra material adds strength and helps prevent the leg from splitting while the mortise is being chopped.

## MORTISE AND TENON ANATOMY

In quality construction the two mortises meet inside the leg. The tenons are mitered so that they nearly meet. (You should aim for about a ¹⁄₁₆" gap between the miters.) The reason for the miter is that it increases the glue area on the outside cheek of the tenon—about 10 percent on most table aprons by my calculations. A 10 percent gain in glue area is significant and worth doing.

The width of a tenon should be about one third the thickness of the apron stock. Since most aprons are likely to be ¾" to ⅞", a ¼" to ½" wide tenon is about right. This leaves the shoulder width somewhere in the neighborhood of ¼" on each side. The set-in is the amount the tenon is set back from the top or bottom of the rail to conceal the joint. This is a

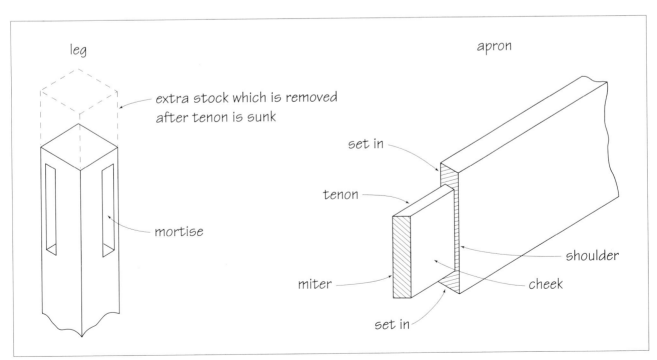

**MODERN MORTISE AND TENON CONSTRUCTION**

completely arbitrary figure and depends much on the worker. Excessive set-in needlessly narrows the tenon which makes the table more susceptible to racking. Generally most workers use around ¼" of set-in (with ⅜" being a maximum) at the top edge of the tenon (where splitting is more likely once the waste is removed) and ⅛" at the bottom. Some workers use little or even no set-in at the bottom. Since only another woodworker is going to lie on the floor and look up at the joint, there is little need to conceal it at the bottom. For reasons of wood movement (see "Wood Movement" on page 67), the tenon must be a bit narrower than the height of the mortise. Therefore, most workers try to have the tenon resting on the bottom of the mortise, leaving the play at the top where it will be concealed by the set-in. Most of the day-to-day forces on the table are downward, and this leaves the tenon well supported and less dependent on the strength of the glue.

The shoulders should be perfectly square and cleanly cut both to the top edge (true edge) and face of the rail. The tenon should be of consistent thickness and should not taper thinner toward the end, or splitting of the leg is likely to result during glue up (or even later when the weather turns damp). Whether cutting by hand or machine, a shoulder rabbet plane is of immense help in squaring up the shoulder. It is also common to cut the tenon too thick, for most workers will error on the

side of safety. Again the shoulder rabbet plane is of great help in thinning the tenon for a proper slide fit.

## HOW WOOD MOVEMENT AFFECTS JOINERY

Let us look in detail at how this wood movement presents a problem in mortise and tenon joinery. As we can see on page 65, the height of the mortise is not going to change because there is no change along the longitudinal grain. The height of the tenon, however, is going to change with humidity—how much depends on grain alignment. If we select quarter-sawn boards, this will be minimized, for we would be dealing with radial expansion and contraction which is less than tangential expansion and contraction. Likewise, the length of the tenon is not going to change with changes in humidity, but the depth of the mortise is—how much depends on the alignment of radial and tangential grains. Therefore, the best grain alignment for a mortise and tenon joint is with a quarter-sawn tenon and the mortise sunk into the tangential grain face. This aligns the radial grain parallel with the depth of the mortise. While quarter-sawn aprons add much to the longevity of the joint, aligning the mortise with the radial grain is hard to achieve in everyday practice. Additionally, it is not as critical, for the mortise depth in the average table leg is seldom great enough to cause drastic problems.

Since dovetails are joints in which

both components are aligned across the grain (see "Drawers and Drawer Construction" on page 99), wood movement is not nearly the problem that it is with mortise and tenons. Since both components tend to move in unison, at more or less the same rate of expansion and contraction, there is little stress put on the glue joint. In fact, the majority of stress to the dovetails in our drawers will come from teenagers who load the drawers unmercifully and open and close them none too gently. Wood movement does present a problem if we employ a solid wood bottom in our drawer. The problem is much the same as that of the table top on the frame, if allowances are not made for expansion and contraction of a solid wood bottom across the grain, it can literally burst the drawer apart at the joints. Solutions to this problem are given in "Drawers and Drawer Construction" on page 99.

Wood movement presents a problem in attaching the top to the frame. Since the longitudinal grain of the aprons sets the size of the frame, we have to make allowances for expansion and contraction across the grain of the top. You will readily see that attaching the top solidly to the frame will invite problems. Usually the top will split down the middle at one or more points. Therefore attachment methods have to make allowances for expansion and contraction. This is covered under "Attaching The Top To The Frame" on page 95.

# Wood Movement

Too often woodworkers think of wood as an inert material much like metal. The truth is, however, that wood is hygroscopic, meaning it absorbs and loses water in relation to changes in the weather. Woe to the woodworker who ignores the changing nature of wood, for he can easily produce work that will destroy itself in short order. Yes, wood has a will of its own.

Complicating the problem, the rates of expansion and contraction are different for longitudinal, radial and tangential grains. Longitudinal movement, expansion and contraction along the grain, is negligible. For the purposes of our discussion it can be considered zero. Radial and tangential movement are, however, significant. Adding to the problem, they are unequal. On average (and this is only an average, for it varies greatly from species to species) the tangential movement is two times the radial movement.

Tangentially sawn plank A yields a wider board but will be more prone to cupping than quarter-sawn plank B. However, in most cases it will have more interesting grain patterns than plank B. Notable exceptions are curly grains, which show better from the radial surface than the tangential surface, and quarter-sawn red oak, which has interesting ray structure that gives flame patterns that can be very beautiful.

Generally speaking, plank A is what we want for tops because of the more interesting grain. We do have to insure that such planks are given equal treatment on both sides if cupping is going to be minimized. Therefore, the underside should be sanded and finished in the same way as the upper surface. This ensures that both sides gain or loose moisture at equal rates and the top remains flat. Leaving the underside of a table top unfinished is inviting problems. By looking at the end of a plank, it is possible to see if it is quartersawn on not. While few planks will exhibit the perfect quartersawing of plank B or C, planks D, E, F and G are reasonably quartersawn and make perfect boards for aprons. We do not have to consider grain direction in legs, for they are square and we will have two tangential and two radial grain faces regardless of how they are sawn.

*Not understanding wood movement was not limited to our time. This davenport desk was made in Ireland in the second half of the nineteenth century and came to my shop for repair. The large check through the top and interior panel is the result of trapping the panels solidly so that they could not move.*

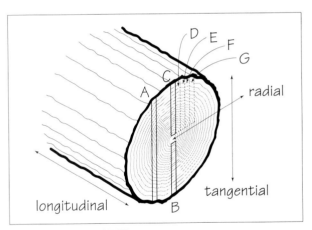

**WOOD MOVEMENT**

A further idiosyncrasy of wood is that only face-grain surfaces glue well. If one or both of two glued wood surfaces are end grain, the only thing we can say for certain is that the glue joint will fail—usually in short order. Therefore, the purpose of all wood joints is to bring face-grain surfaces together to create glue area. However, a glue joint in which the face grains are at right angles to each other is more prone to problems due to expansion and contraction than one in which the face grains are aligned. A mortise and tenon exhibits the former while a dovetail joint exhibits the latter.

# HAND CUT MORTISE AND TENONS

For those lacking the machinery to machine cut tenons hand cutting offers a good cheap alternative. The only tools required are a mortise chisel of the proper size, a back saw, a square, a ruler and a mortising gauge. Other than the ruler and square, none of these tools are available at the average local hardware store. There are a variety of mail-order sources which offer these products, however.

*I have definite preferences when it comes to mortise chisels and back saws. I like a London pattern mortise chisel which is offered by a number of English and Continental manufacturers. The chisel on the left is by Stanley (made by their Goldburg Division in France), and the right example is by Nooitegadgt (Holland). While a set of mortise chisels is nice, those on a budget can get by nicely with only a ⁵⁄₁₆" width which will cover all aprons from ¾" to ⅞" thick. The back saw is the Ultimate Back Saw which is a Japanese saw that cuts on the push stroke in a Western Style.*

## MAKING THE MORTISE

**STEP 1**

## Select the Chisel

The first task is to select a chisel which should be about one third the thickness of the apron material. A ¼" or ⁵⁄₁₆" width is good for ¾" aprons while ⁵⁄₁₆" or ½" is best for ⅞" to 1" aprons. Set the mortising gauge to the width of the chisel and adjust the fence for the proper placement of the mortise on the leg.

**STEP 1**

## Mark Out the Mortise

Mark the two sides of the leg which will be exposed on the outside of the table; these will be the true faces. Use a square to mark the waste portion, which will be cut away after the mortise is chopped. Align the apron with the bottom of the waste and make a mark to show the width of the tenon. Set the mortising gauge for the width of the chisel. Place the fence of the mortising gauge against each face and mark out the sides of the mortise between the two marks.

**STEP 2**

## Mark the Waste Area

Measure the set-in and mark this out. Scribble the waste area so that there can be no mistakes as where to chop.

**STEP 3**

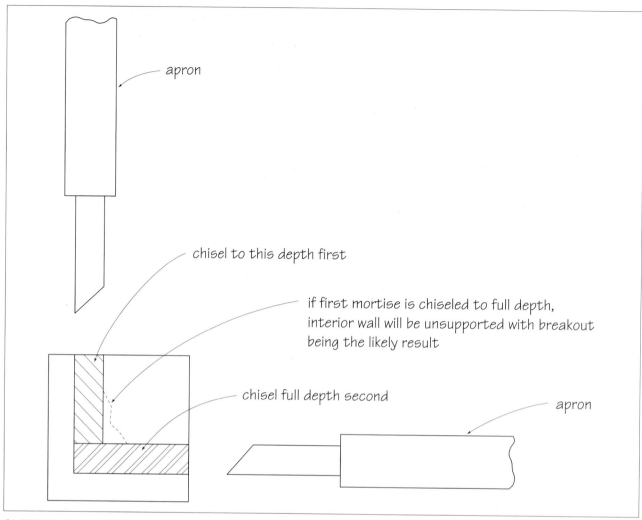

apron

chisel to this depth first

if first mortise is chiseled to full depth, interior wall will be unsupported with breakout being the likely result

chisel full depth second

apron

**CUTTING SEQUENCE**

*Sequence of cutting to avoid internal breakout of mortises that meet inside a leg.*

## STEP 4

# Mark the Mortise Depth

Place the chisel on the laid out tenon and tape it ⅛" more than the length of the tenon. This ensures that the tenon will be deeper than the mortise. If the leg is to have two mortises, the first one will have to be cut to a lesser depth as shown above.

**STEP 4**

**STEP 5**

STEP 5

# Secure the Leg

Clamp the leg securely to the bench. Make a series of light cuts between the two layout lines.

**STEP 6**

STEP 6

# Begin Cutting the Mortise

Use the chisel to sweep away the raised chips. This will now allow you to easily place the chisel between the two lines.

# Chisel to Depth

Start in the middle of the mortise and alternately chisel downward in an area just wider than the chisel until you are to the depth marked by the tape. The idea is to chisel down as far as possible and lever the chips out. Do not enlarge the center portion more than you have to until you are to full depth.

**STEP 7**

**LOCK MORTISING CHISEL**

*A lock mortising chisel is very handy for leaving out the waste when starting the mortises. This was a comon tool up through the nineteenth century, but it is no longer available. I made this one from an old Allen wrench.*

**STEP 8**

# Lever Out the Waste

After you are to full depth, progress to each end of the mortise in ⅟₁₆" to ⅛" increments. The idea is to chisel down to the taped depth and lever the waste up and out. Check that the chisel is square to the work each time you start it.

**STEP 9**

# Make Final Cuts

On the last cut, lever forward and not backward so as not to round over the edge. The lock mortise chisel can be used to lever this last waste out.

**THE FINISHED MORTISE**

*By this correct classical method, the mortise can never be wider than the chisel and will be of constant width. Some texts suggest drilling a series of holes, but I disagree with this. On small mortises one central hole aids chiseling down to depth, any more leads to one or both sides of the mortise being scalloped and the glue area suffering.*

## SAWING THE TENON

**STEP 1**

# Prepare to Mark the Tenon

Readjust the marking gage fence (being very careful to keep the two scribes at the width of the mortising chisel used to cut the mortise in the leg) so as to center the two marks in the middle of the apron. This does not have to be exact center, only center by eye.

**STEP 1**

**STEP 2**

## Mark the Tenon

Mark the then length by scribing around the apron with a square. Some workers use a bench knife for this, and I prefer this method, for it leaves a very clean shoulder so tear out by the saw is minimized. Always mark from the face side and top edge (true edge) of the apron.

**STEP 2**

**STEP 3**

## Transfer the Set in Distances from the Mortise

Place the end of the apron on the mortise and transfer the set-in distances. Remember to add ⅟₁₆" to the top dimension so that the tenon width will be ⅟₁₆" less than the mortise height.

**STEP 3**

# Cut the Tenon Cheeks

Place the apron vertically in a vice and rip the cheeks with a back saw. Be careful to cut exactly on the line, but to the waste side of the line. The saw should split your layout line. The idea is to mark carefully and to work to the layout lines so that the tenon fits the mortise right off of the saw. The tendency is to always cut oversize, a tendency you should resist. Cut just to the tenon length but not past it.

**STEP 4**

# Cut the Set In

Next, rip the set-ins.

**STEP 5**

**STEP 6**

# Cut the Tenon Shoulders

Cut the shoulders, again with the saw to the waste side and splitting the lay out lines. A bench hook like the one in use is easy to make and immensely useful for this task. It holds the apron securely while protecting the bench.

**STEP 7**

# Cut the Shoulder Set-Ins

Cut the set-in

# Clean Up the Tenon

Clean up the shoulders with a shoulder rabbet plane. If the tenon is too wide, trim the cheeks with the shoulder rabbet plane.

**STEP 8**

# Cut the Miter

If the tenon is to be mitered, the easiest way to do it is with a plane and a donkey's ear shooting board.

**STEP 9**

**THE FINISHED MORTISE AND TENON**

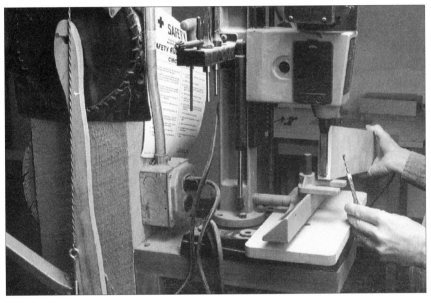

**STEP 1**

# MAKING MORTISE AND TENONS WITH A MORTISER AND TABLE SAW

A hollow chisel mortising machine is a quick and sure way to cut mortises. The heart of the machine is a hollow square chisel with an auger bit which turns inside of it. The drill bores ahead, and the chisel follows trimming the hole square. The machine literally drills a square hole. While most drill presses can be fitted with hollow chisels, dedicated machines, such as the one shown in the following sequences, offer more leverage. A good deal of force is necessary to drive the chisel. While a drill press can handle the job, the lack of leverage will make the job tiring, especially if there are a number of large mortises to cut.

## CHOPPING THE MORTISE

### STEP 1
## Select a Chisel

The first task is to select a hollow chisel that is about one third the thickness of the apron. For most tables, ¼" (for ¾" aprons) or ½" (for ⅞" to 1" aprons) will be about right. This chisel will dictate the size of the mortise and so also dictates the thickness of the tenon.

# Set Mortise Depth

Set the chisel to the proper depth. If the leg has two mortises which meet, the first one will have to be drilled to a lesser depth to prevent internal breakout as shown on page 70.

**STEP 2**

# Cut the Mortise

On the first cut, it is going to be difficult to pull the chisel back out because all four sides are buried. Waxing or spraying silicone on the chisel periodically helps greatly with this problem. Chisel with overlapping cuts. At least half the chisel should be cutting at all times or it will drift away from the cut. If the final cut is going to be less than half the chisel, then cut the end of the mortise first; then center the chisel over the remaining web for the final cut.

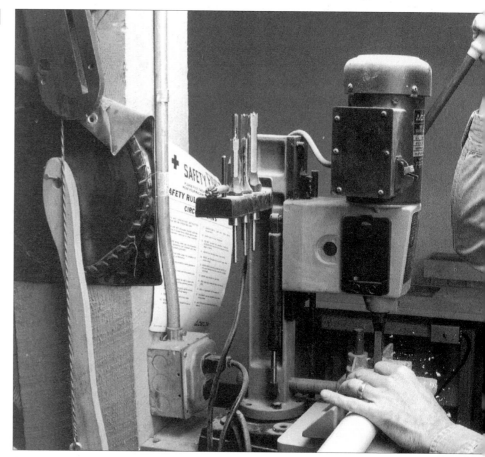

**STEP 3**

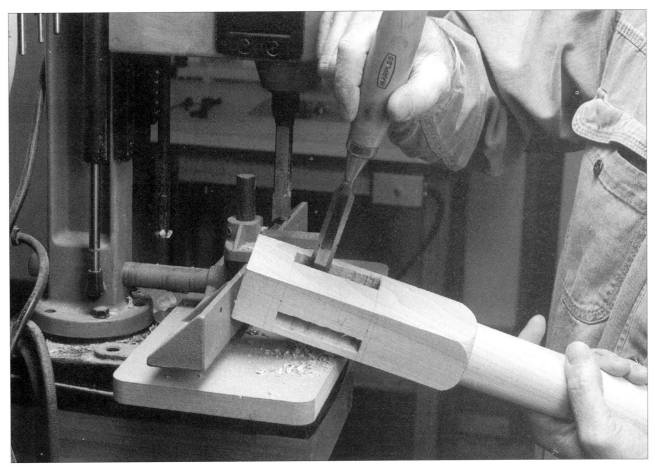

**THE FINISHED MORTISE**

A tenon raising jig, such as the one shown in the photo, is the best way to raise a tenon. It allows secure holding of the stock while keeping hands safe. Because the splitter and guard usually have to be removed for tenoning operations, great care should be exercised. Under no circumstances should tenons be attempted without a tenoning jig. Commercial jigs are reasonably priced, or the jig can be shop-built.

**TENONING JIG**

## MAKING THE TENON ON THE TABLE SAW

STEP 1

# Cut the Tenon Cheeks

The first job is to cut the cheeks of the tenon. For machine-cut tenons, it is helpful to have all the stock the exact same thickness. Therefore, apron stock should be jointed and planed as a batch, and no hand planing or sanding should be done before the tenon is cut. Have extra material for setup and make test cuts to get everything accurate. Some adjustment of the jig is necessary to get things perfect. Each cheek of the tenon is cut individually, and for this reason any adjustment of the jig is doubled reference change in tenon thickness. (If many tenons are to be cut, tenon bushings in conjunction with two saw blades allow cutting both cheeks in one pass. Most manufacturers sell tenon bushings sized to their hollow mortise chisels.) Carefully adjust the saw blade to the shoulder mark, which is the length of the tenon.

STEP 2

# Cut Tenon Shoulders

The shoulder is cut next, so adjust the blade to the shoulder width. A stop is set to the tenon length so that the blade trims exactly on the shoulder. Notice that the table-saw fence is not used directly as a stop for this operation, but rather a block is clamped to the fence as a stop. The former will result in nasty kickbacks from the loose piece as it drops away. This can be quite dangerous.

**STEP 1**

**STEP 2**

**STEP 3**

STEP 3

# Cut the Set Ins

Adjust the blade to the set-in distance and use the same set up as for the shoulders to cut the set-in.

**STEP 4**

STEP 4

# Rip the Set In Waste

I find the easiest way to rip the set-in waste is with a band saw.

# Miter the Tenon

If the tenon is to be mitered, set the
table saw blade to 45 degrees and
cut the miter.

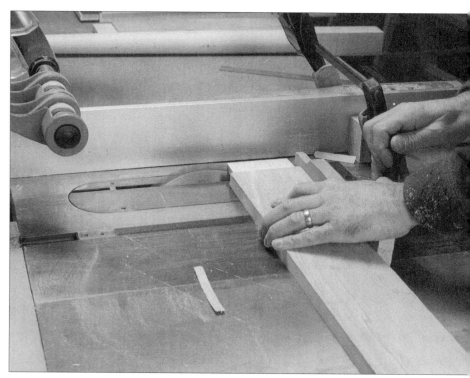

**STEP 3**

**THE FINISHED MORTISE AND TENON**

# PINNED MORTISE AND TENON JOINTS

We are all familiar with the wooden cross pins used in timber frame construction. The mortise and tenon joints in timber frame construction are not glued but mechanically pinned together. Because of the likelihood of a glue failure in mortise and tenon joints, it was common to cross pin them in furniture as well. The practice is seen frequently in real Queen Anne furniture and the Shakers did it routinely. Most doors from the colonial period were not glued at all, but rather pinned and/or wedged. One only has to try to take such a door apart to realize how strong mechanical fastening is.

Most woodworkers only pin a joint today to be faithful to a certain style of furniture, such as Queen Anne or Shaker. However, a properly cross pinned joint adds much in strength, ensuring that even if the glue fails the joint will not. If the cross pinning is going to be more than cosmetic, then the tenon needs to be long enough that there is no likelihood of the wood breaking along the grain in back of where the cross hole is drilled. Timber framers would say "there needs to be enough relish in the tenon."

Cross pins were usually split out, or riven, so that all the grain fibers were parallel, then whittled to a gentle taper. A cross hole was drilled through the joint and the pin driven home. The excess was then pared off with a sharp chisel.

## PINNING A MORTISE AND TENON JOINT

**STEP 1**

## Drill Holes for the Pins

Cross drill the joint. Two pins, spaced at thirds across the tenon, are almost always used. If the leg has two tenons, the cross holes in one tenon should be at a different height that the other so as not to excessively weaken the leg.

## STEP 2

# Whittle the Pins

Whittle a slightly tapered pin from scrap wood from the project. Tap pins into each of the holes. Do not pound; only tap gently, so as not to split the leg. The taper will cause the pin to lock permanently.

**STEP 2**

## STEP 3

# Trim Off the Excess

Pare away the excess with a sharp bench chisel.

**STEP 3**

**THE DOWELING JIG**

*A doweling jig with a dowel joint. Dowel joints can also be easily made.*

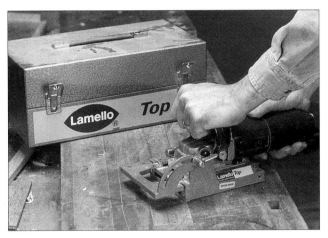

**PLATE JOINTER**

*Plate joinery is easily accomplished with one of the many compact, portable plate joining machines available today.*

**PLATE JOINT**

*Plate joints are far superior to dowel joints because they have large amounts of face-grain glue area, are always aligned perfectly reference the face of the work, and have ⅛" of adjustment in the other axes.*

# USING DOWELED JOINERY

During the industrial revolution the need for mass produced furniture, combined with complexity in producing proper mortise and tenon joints, made furnituremakers look for cheaper, faster alternatives. The first of these was the dowel joint. While not as strong as a mortise and tenon, the dowel joint is readily made by machinery and is used extensively (even today) in mass produced furniture. In the dowel joint, the apron ends in a butt joint against the leg; holes are drilled in both pieces and then held together with glued dowels. The heart of the dowel joint is machinery or jigs that make placement of drilled holes in exact juxtaposition possible.

Dowel joints are easily made with the minimum of tooling. An electric (or even hand-powered) drill and a doweling jig is all you need. Doweled joints have little strength because there is very little flat grain to flat grain glue area. This joint is extensively used in face frame cabinetry.

# USING BISCUIT JOINERY

Properly called plate joinery, biscuit joinery is a splendid alternative to dowel joints and to a lesser extent mortise and tenon joints. The idea was conceived in the 1950s by a Swiss cabinetmaker, Herman Steiner, who was dissatisfied with the dowel joint. Besides the face-grain glue-area problem of dowel joints, they are difficult to execute consistently because of the problem of aligning two holes perfectly in two axes. The plate joint overcomes this problem by using a small 4" diameter saw blade to cut a $\frac{5}{32}$" wide circular kerf which accepts an elliptical wood plate. The result is a joint that is always aligned perfectly reference the face of the work and has ⅛" of adjustment in the other axes. This means that the apron can be aligned perfectly with the leg, but can slide up or down to align perfectly with the top of the leg before the glue sets. In essence it is an adjustable joint. It is also far superior to a dowel joint for two reasons. The first is that there is a far better face-grain glue area. The second is that the plate is compressed during manufacture so that it swells in the kerf as it adsorbs the glue. The result is that the joint seldom needs clamping after about ten minutes, the plate has swollen sufficiently to hold everything fast until the glue dries.

# USING KNOCKDOWN HARDWARE

Sometimes it is necessary to be able to remove the legs from a table. For those who move a lot, have stairways and doorways that prohibit passage of an assembled table, or want a table that will store away the majority of the time, knockdown construction is the way to go. There is hardware to solve this problem, and construction is dictated by the brand used. Most employ bolts and wing nuts to hold.

# USING CROSS BRACING FOR LONGER TABLES

Longer tables such as dining tables often require intermediate cross bracing of the frame for added strength. The exact nature of the cross bracing will vary with the nature of the table. It can vary from through wedged tenons to simple crosspieces screwed to blocks glued to the back sides of the aprons. There is no set solution, and anything that cures the problem and allows for wood movement without spoiling the design is fine.

**KNOCKDOWN JOINTS**
*A variety of hardware is available that allows knockdown construction.*

# MAKING TABLE TOPS

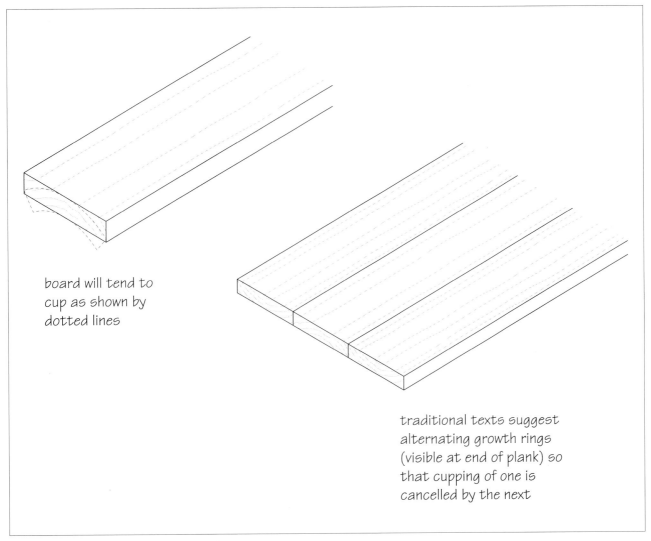

board will tend to cup as shown by dotted lines

traditional texts suggest alternating growth rings (visible at end of plank) so that cupping of one is cancelled by the next

**STRATEGIES FOR GLUING UP TOPS**

The top is the essence of the table, for it is the part seen most and what that friendly cup of coffee is ultimately going to sit on. The sad truth is that the average person is not going to see the fine joinery; for once glued up, mortise and tenon joints are completely hidden. The average viewer expects good design, sanding and finish, but a top with exceptional wood grain is going to

stop them in their tracks. In short the top is what is going to bring the "ohs" and "ahs" more than anything else. By understanding wood and selecting it carefully, we can achieve a top that will make our table an heirloom.

As we learned in the sidebar "Wood Movement" on page 67, tangentially sawn plank A is what we generally want for a table top.

Notable exceptions are curly grains which show better from the radial surface than the tangential surface, and quarter-sawn red oak which has interesting ray structure that give beautiful flame patterns. However our tangentially sawn plank will be more prone to cupping than quarter-sawn plank B, especially if it absorbs or loses greater amounts of moisture from one side than the other.

# GLUING UP TOPS

Most tops will require that two or more boards be glued together to get sufficient width. There are conflicting strategies for gluing boards together. The traditional strategy is to alternate the growth rings as shown on page 89. The thinking goes that the cupping of each board will cancel the cupping of the next. Actually we are going to joint and plane the boards flat, and they will remain that way unless they gain or lose moisture unequally from the two sides. If dry lumber is selected and equal treatment is given to both sides, cupping is going to be minimized. Therefore, it is more important that the underside should be sanded and finished in the same way as the upper surface, than how we arrange the boards. This ensures that both sides gain or lose moisture at equal rates and the top remains flat. Leaving the underside of a table top unfinished is inviting problems.

With this in mind, I select the glue up pattern on the basis of face grains and do not worry about how the growth rings fall. I pick the most interesting side and arrange the boards for the most interesting combination of patterns. I then ensure that equal treatment is given to both sides throughout the rest of the building process.

The most important factor in gluing up a top is to get first-rate glue joints between he boards. All that is necessary is to have straight square surfaces on both sides of the joint. This can be done with a O7 or O8 hand jointer plane, a power jointer, or a combination of both. Since all jointers leave some ripple, I always take a final pass or two with a jointer plane after machine jointing because the resulting super-straight, smooth surface gives me a nearly invisible glue joint.

## TOP MATERIAL

I like to make my tops from 5/4 material because this gives me a finished top that is between ⅞" and 1" thick. Many modern workers tend to use ¾" material for tops and they look puny. Antique tables almost always exhibit thicker material, and this is one of the many reasons why we revere such furniture. What is more, the thicker material will be more likely to remain flat.

While I use the traditional hide glue in my mortise and tenon joints and dovetails, I generally use cold glue (such as Titebond or Elmers) for glue joints in table tops. Since the grain in these edge joints is aligned in the same way wood movement (see the sidebar "Wood Movement" on page 67) is not going to be a problem. Therefore, cold glue is much more convenient. Resist the temptation to use dowels, plates or splices in these glue joints. There is no need, for we are gluing face grain to face grain and as long as we have true surfaces the glue joint will be stronger than the wood no matter what glue we use. Simply spread liberal amounts of glue, align the pieces carefully and clamp until the glue dries.

**STEP 4**

## GLUING UP A TOP

STEP 1

## Mark the Stock

Start with wood ¼" thicker than you need. (See section on "Milling Square Lumber" on page 44 for information on buying lumber.) Face joint each board to get it flat and true. Mark this "true face" and joint one edge square to the true face. Mark this "true edge." If you lack a jointer wide enough to do this task, you can have the mill do it or use a hand plane.

**STEP 2**

## Plane the Stock

Plane the second side of each board parallel to the true face. Start with the thickest board and plane each board in turn until they are all clean and true. They will now all be the same thickness.

**STEP 3**

## Square Up the Top

On the table saw, rip a second side parallel to the true edge. Joint the second edge once ripped.

**STEP 4**

## Joint the Next Edge

Hand plane the jointed edge with a jointer bench plane (O7 or O8) if you wish. Trial fit each board to ensure that there is a perfect fit. If there is not, re-joint and/or re-hand plane as necessary to achieve a perfect fit.

## STEP 5

# Glue Up the Edge

Apply a generous line of glue to the board.

**STEP 5**

## STEP 6

# Apply Clamps

Place the boards together in the proper juxtaposition and clamp. The clamps should alternate so as to even stress. Allow to dry 2 to 24 hours depending on the glue used.

**STEP 6**

**THE RULE JOINT**
*A rule joint is commonly used to attach a drop leaf to the main part of the top.*

**RULE JOINT BITS**
*A matched set of router bits, called a rule joint set, is used to cut the rule joint for a drop leaf.*

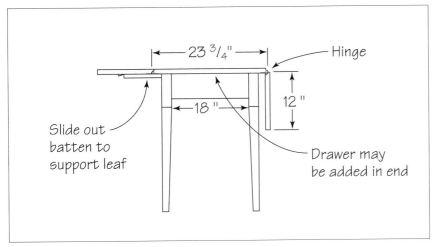

**ADDING A DROP LEAF**
*A drop leaf is the solution when you desire to have a small table most of the time but need a wider table occasionally. One or both leaves may be raised when needed.*

## EDGE TREATMENT

An important part of the design statement of any table is the treatment given the edges of the top. This can vary from simply leaving the edge square, but planed and sanded smooth, to milling of complicated molded shapes. With today's wide selection of router bits, options abound. For smaller tops the router table may make precise milling easier, while for large tops, hand holding the router usually works better. If hand holding the router a fence is a must.

## USING DROP LEAVES

It is often desirable to put a drop leaf in a table top. Drop leaves allow a large top area, a good part of which can be folded out of the way to aid traffic flow or gain floor space. Drop leaves are common on end, side and dining tables. Metal hinges are normally inleted to the underside of the top and leaf to allow the leaf to fold down along the side of the frame. While the leaf may be butt jointed to the main top, a rule joint, such as shown in  is more commonly used. This joint derives its name from four-fold folding wood rules and was originally cut with a set of matched molding planes. Today it is better cut with a matched set of router bits as shown in. (See sources of supply for rule joint router bits.) A rule joint better keeps the drop leaf and top in alignment with day-to-day changes in humidity and makes a perfect, light tight, fit when the leaf is raised.

## DROP LEAF SUPPORT

Some means of supporting the leaf must be devised. A folding knee like the one shown in is often used. A knee will support very heavy loads. While the hinge in this fine antique example was created through joinery a metal hinge is commonly employed today. A more common solution, because it is easier, is a pull out, or swing out, wood batten to support the leaf.

**SUPPORTING KNEE**
*This antique mahogany veneered Empire table has a beautifully crafted knee with an all wood hinge inleted into the frame. This table was built at the cusp of the machine age and is a hand tool tour de force.*

**MAKING A KNEE**
*I crafted this knee for the leaf on my kitchen island after the knee in the Empire table. It was a fun joinery project, mostly done with a band saw and a disc sander.*

**A SIMPLE SUPPORT**
*A much simpler support is a pull-out or swing-out wood batten to support the leaf.*

**INCORRECT TOP ATTACHMENT**
*This is an example of what happens when an unknowing worker attaches a top solidly to the frame. This top was doweled to the trestle, and the large cracks are the result.*

**MORTISE BUTTONS**

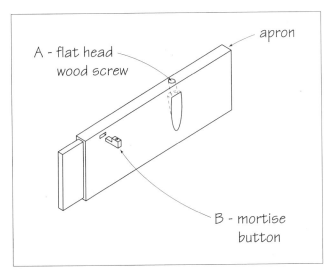

**SCREWS AND MORTISE BUTTONS**

## ATTACHING THE TOP TO THE FRAME

Because of wood movement (see the sidebar "Wood Movement" on page 67), the top cannot be affixed rigidly to the frame. Therefore, the top has to be affixed in such a way that it is held down but can slide on the frame when it expands and contracts. The three principal methods are screws, mortise buttons and commercial hardware. They all essentially achieve the same end.

You may be familiar with commercial hardware that is used to attach table tops to aprons. This uses the same principle as the mortise buttons employing stamped steel angle pieces instead of the wooden buttons. The materials are different but the principle is the same.

# CHAPTER SEVEN

# MAKING TABLE DRAWERS

It is hard to pinpoint the exact date in history that we began to employ drawers in tables. Since early times tables have included one or more drawers. They add handy storage to what would otherwise be wasted space. Adding a drawer complicates construction considerably, but it is well worth the effort. What's more, the drawer front and pull can add much to the design statement of the table. A drawer is pure carcass construction. A carcass is basically a box.

## DRAWER JOINERY

As outlined in "Wood Movement" on page 67, joining the corners of the box together presents a problem. Since we cannot glue end grain, joints that bring face-grain glue areas into contact must be employed. The dovetail is the classical solution to this problem, but since the beginning of the nineteenth century, various machine-cut alternatives, such as lock joints, pin and scallop joints or machine-cut dovetails have be used successfully.

This shows a classically constructed drawer. It has half blind dovetails at the front, through dovetails at the back, and a solid wood bottom trapped in a groove running around the front and sides. The solid wood bottom has the longitudinal grain running across the drawer. Expansion and contraction of the bottom is across the grain, so

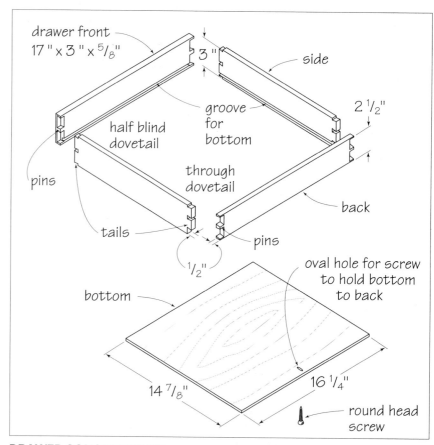

**DRAWER CONSTRUCTION**

movement will only be a problem from front to back in the drawer. During installation the bottom is not pushed all the way to the bottom of the front groove and is attached with nails, or better yet, screws to the back. This allows the bottom to expand and contract in the front groove.

Most American woodworkers mill the groove for the bottom directly into the side of the drawer as shown in figure A of page 97. The problem with this approach is that

as the bottom of the drawer wears, the support for the bottom will become progressively less. After years of use, the entire piece below the groove breaks away. This is a common occurrence judging by how many antiques I have seen with strips glued in this area. Therefore, I favor a technique worked out in Europe in the early part of this century. By this method the groove is not let directly into the side of the drawer. Rather a drawer slip, with the groove milled in it, is glued to the inside of the front and sides. This approach allows a much thinner drawer side, adding much to good design. The strips add extra width to the drawer sides, adding to longevity because of the extra wear surface. Two variations of this approach are illustrated in figures B and C (below). The first is for small drawers where an absolutely flat bottom is desired (e.g., for storage of papers, etc.). The second is stronger because of the larger groove and is the variation I most often use for table drawers. Such things as games or table linen are most often stored in table drawers, and the rounded edge of the drawer slip does not interfere with these.

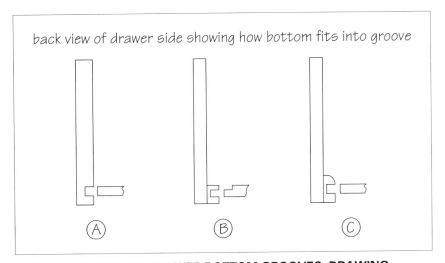

**PIN AND SCALLOP JOINERY**

*The pin and scallop was very popular during the high Victorian Period. It required highly specialized machinery, but it was probably stronger than dovetails judging by how many have survived intact. There are specialized jigs that are available to today's woodworkers to make these joints.*

## DRAWER BOTTOMS

Today plywood or Masonite is usually substituted for solid wood as a bottom material. Neither changes size much with changes in humidity, and plywood is stronger than solid wood. Since there is no need to allow for dimensional changes with such materials, many workers elect to make the back the same height as the rest of the drawer and to trap the bottom in a groove running around the four sides. If plywood is used, the grain should run across the drawer to retain a classical look and feel. While it does not really matter which way the grain runs, this is the traditional way.

## HAND CUT DOVETAIL JOINTS

Hand-cut dovetails are the mark of fine furniture. With a bit of practice, they are easy to cut—in fact, I find cutting dovetails to be rather therapeutic. I like to cut them after dinner to Mozart, for some reason. Some workers are quite dogmatic about whether you should cut the pins or the tails first. In reality, it does not

**back view of drawer side showing how bottom fits into groove**

Ⓐ    Ⓑ    Ⓒ

**DIFFERENT TYPES OF DRAWER BOTTOM GROOVES  DRAWING**

matter which you do first. The main thing is to have a sharp backsaw and chisels, to layout carefully, and always cut to the waste side of the line. If you do these things, the dovetail should fit as cut, which is the idea. The finished joint should be a press fit, but hand-cut dovetails should never actually be assembled until actual glue up for dry fitting; it will spoil the press fit.

## MACHINE CUT DOVETAIL JOINTS

Dovetails may also be machine cut, and numerous jigs are available that are used in conjunction with a router. One can spend anywhere from $30 to $350 on such a jig. Jigs on the lower end of the price scale generally only cut half blind dovetails. Better jigs cut both, while the best jigs are also adjustable as to pin spacing. After assembly, dovetails cut with such jigs are virtually impossible to tell from hand cut. Inexpensive, half blind only, jigs are available at Sears and home centers. Jigs that allow great flexibility are the Lee Jig and the Omni Jig. The router table in conjunction with a precision fence adjusting system, such as the Incra Jig or the IPM Machine, allow cutting of both half blind and through dovetails at any pin spacing. I think the process of using the router table and these systems for such an end is as much or more trouble than hand cutting. See Sources of Supply for jig sources.

## DOVETAIL ANATOMY

The dovetail not only brings face-grain glue surfaces into contact with each other; it is also a mechanical joint in one axis. Since the stress of opening and closing the drawer will be on the front and back of the drawer (e.g., one teenager puts 100 lb. of "stuff" in the drawer, opens it violently and slams it shut shaking the entire table), the tails are cut into the drawer sides with the pins in the front and back. This puts the mechanical strength of the dovetail in line with the stress. The lock miter joint is also a mechanical joint in one axis, just as the dovetail.

## DRAWER FRONTS

Drawers are either flush face or overlay face, meaning that the drawer is an exact fit in the opening and closes flush with the face of the apron or is slightly bigger than the opening and closes onto the face of the opening. The latter requires some type of edge treatment such as a quarter round to break the transition from the drawer face to the apron. A flush face needs a drawer stop for proper alignment while an overlay face doesn't need a stop.

*For drawers in utility and work tables, commercial metal slides are a good solution. They support large amounts of weight, limit opening, and many allow self-closing features if desired. Generally about ½" additional clearance is necessary at the sides so the design only works well with an overlay face.*

## DRAWER MATERIAL

A failing of many modern workers is to build a drawer entirely out of ¾" material. This makes for a chunky drawer. For most tables a drawer front that is between ⅝" and ⅞" thick with sides and backs that are ⅜" to ½" thick works out about right. This provides more than enough strength (especially if drawer slips are employed for the groove), while retaining a dainty, refined look to the drawer.

## DRAWER SLIDES

In the words of English cabinetmaker Cecil Gough, "A well fitting drawer can be likened to a piston working in a cylinder. For a drawer to fit well, not only is it important that the drawer itself is absolutely accurate on the outside, but equally important is the accuracy of the opening into which it must slide." Drawer slides are the frame work which provide this opening—in short they are the cylinder. On fine furniture the drawer slides are wood strips attached to the inside of the frame. They provide a runway for the drawer itself, limiting side-to-side and up-and-down movement. Complicating the problem, they should be a bit wider at the back of the drawer than at the front. The top of the table often provides the top support in this regard. Proper drawer slides can be an engineering problem. Fortunately, on most tables they can easily be glued to the inside edges of the apron.

## DRAWER STOPS

Drawer stops align the face of the drawer with the face of the apron when the drawer is fully closed. In most tables small blocks of wood glued to the cross member below the drawer provide excellent stops. Stops at the back of the drawer are difficult to work out and can be a problem with solid bottoms due to expansion and contraction of the bottom changing the stop point. An idea of how to go about solving these details is shown in the section that follows.

**STEP 1**

# MAKING A DRAWER

The following shows the building of the drawer for the Empire End Table shown on page 2. These techniques will work for building just about any drawer. Refer to the exploded drawing on page 10 for this particular drawer.

## BUILDING A DRAWER

**STEP 1**

# Mark the Stock

Now we will turn our attention to the drawer. For most joints the drawer front should be thicker than the sides and back. If machine-cut half blind dovetails or a lock miter joint is to be used, the back generally needs to be the same thickness as the front. Start by arranging all of the pieces (which should all be very slightly oversize) in the correct juxtaposition and mark with carpenter's triangles. These simple marks will allow aligning any two pieces in the proper orientation at any time.

**STEP 2**

# Trial Fit Parts

Trial fit each piece with the slides. I often set a piece of plywood, or the actual top, in place if it is to be the top of the slides.

**STEP 2**

## Cut the Joinery

Cut the joints that are going to join the drawer together, in this case hand-cut dovetails. I am transferring the pin pattern to the sides for cutting of the tails.

**STEP 3**

## Mill Drawer Bottom Groove

Mill the groove for the bottom. My preference for this task is a router table and a ¼" spiral fluted router bit. I make the half pins at the top and bottom of the front small enough that the groove clears them. This generally means that the half pin dimension is less than ¼".

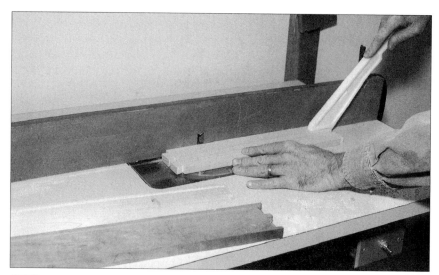

**STEP 4**

## Glue Up the Drawer

Glue up the drawer. It is best to check squareness with a try square.

**STEP 5**

**STEP 6**

STEP 6

# Install the Bottom

Once the glue dries, cut the bottom to exact size and install it.

**STEP 7**

STEP 7

# Set the Bottom

Make sure that the bottom does not bottom out in the front groove. While early American workers usually nailed the bottom to the back, a screw and an elongated hole is a more elegant solution. No matter what the humidity, the bottom can move without causing structural damage to the carcass. I like to use a brass round head screw here.

**STEP 8**

STEP 8

# Fit the Drawer

Clean up the drawer with a hand plane or sander.

# Install the Knob

Install the knob and you are done
with the drawer.

**STEP 9**

# Install the Drawer
Slides

Install the drawer slides. They are
glued to the insides of the apron and
are generally built up out of two
pieces. They can be clamped or
nailed until the glue dries.

**STEP 10**

**STEP 11**

# Use Feelers to Fit the Drawer Slides

They should be a bit wider at the back than at the front (for most table drawers ½₂" per side or ¹⁄₁₆" total is a good figure). A good way to gauge this is to cut a strip of wood the exact width of the front opening and use this as a feeler gauge at various points to the back of the slide.

**STEP 12**

# Install the Drawer Stops

Install the drawer stops at the right distance from the apron front.

# Install the Drawer

Install the drawer. I like to crayon paraffin on the slides and drawer to make for a smooth running fit.

# MAKING DRAWER PULLS

A drawer pull, or knob, is an important element, both from a utility and a design standpoint. A good pull allows easy opening of the drawer and furthers the design statement of the table. Furthermore, it does not work loose easily. For utility and work tables, kitchen cabinet pulls available at most hardware stores will do fine. Fine furniture demands solid brass, wrought iron or hand-turned pulls. Being a turner, I like to turn my own pulls. They can be of scrap wood left from the legs and so match the table. A personal signature as of late is to set a dot of contrasting wood in the center of my hand turned knob. Finding good commercial pulls, especially for period furniture such as Queen Anne, can be difficult and expensive. See Sources of Supply for pull sources.

A very good option is no pull at all. By routing a cove in the bottom edge of the drawer, the drawer front becomes a pull. This is a good option in dining tables because it makes the drawer unobtrusive. The drawer slides do have to be engineered differently for this scheme to work.

**STEP 13**

**PULL STYLES**

*The drawer at left and center have hand-turned pulls. The left one has an inlaid center dot of contrasting wood which is a personal signature as of late. The drawer at right is from a dining table by Kelly Mehler. It has no pull at all but rather a cove routed in the bottom to provide purchase.*

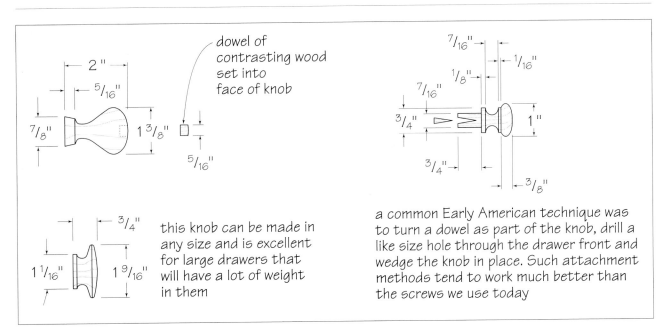

dowel of contrasting wood set into face of knob

2 "

5/16"

7/8"

1 3/8"

5/16"

3/4"

1 1/16"

1 9/16"

this knob can be made in any size and is excellent for large drawers that will have a lot of weight in them

7/16"

1/16"

7/16"

1/8"

3/4"

1"

3/4"

3/8"

a common Early American technique was to turn a dowel as part of the knob, drill a like size hole through the drawer front and wedge the knob in place. Such attachment methods tend to work much better than the screws we use today

**HAND TURNED PULL STYLES**

# CHAPTER EIGHT

# FINISHING TABLES

The number of finishing products available today boggles the mind. My reasons for using them are success, ease of application and safety. I do not own a spray gun so all of my finishes are hand applied.

Finishing is a subject woodworkers talk about endlessly. And for good reason, it is the step in the building process that can make or break a table. In fact I think of finishing as a metamorphosis in which a caterpillar becomes a butterfly. It is also the stage where we, as craftspeople, can make our table stand out from the store-bought variety. As mentioned in the discussion on buying lumber in the section on page 44, furniture factories use only select wood which has plain grain. They further hide wood color mismatching, imperfections and defects by finishing with lacquer that actually has stain mixed in it. The resulting rather opaque finish hides the otherwise boring wood. In the worst cases, further "character" is provided in a process called distressing where dark lacquer is randomly splattered onto the surface to give an antique look. The whole effect certainly distresses me! We can apply a clear finish that will bring out the best our lower grade, but more "interesting," wood has to offer. Finishing is an area where most of us lack knowledge. We tend to have one or two pet finishes that work and leave it at that. An ideal finish should be transparent, so as to enhance the beauty of the wood, while at the same time protecting it from water, dirt, grease and oil. Finishing can be divided into four distinct stages: surface preparation, staining, filling and applying the actual finish. It is outside the scope of this book to be a course in finishing; so I, like most woodworkers, will share my favorite finishes.

# SURFACE PREPARATION

Surface preparation is a vital step in the finishing process and yet the area most often given short shrift. Small wonder, for who likes sanding? Unfortunately the final finish will only be as good as the surface you start with, so it is worth spending sufficient time on this important first step. Sanding to a uniform surface is imperative. How fine depends on the final finish (and type of finish) you desire. Obviously it would be silly to put a high-gloss finish on a work table so sanding to 120- or 180-grit sandpaper makes sense. For a high-gloss finish sanding to a minimum of 220-grit is imperative.

Excessive power sanding with coarse grits usually leads to washed out edges and low spots. That is why I do my initial surface preparation with a very sharp, well tuned hand plane. This gives me level surfaces with crisp edge detail. What is more, there is no dust or noise. Next, I can start sanding at 180-grit, which I generally do with a random-orbit sander with a vacuum attachment built into it. My final sanding is always by hand with the grain.

## USING STAINS

Stains lend color to the wood and can actually be divided into dyes and pigments. Dyes sink into the wood and change its color from within. Pigmented stains are like a thin paint. They form a thin coating on the wood and trick the eye into seeing color. My preference is for dyes on light colored, close grained woods, such as maple and birch. Most commercial stains are pigmented type consisting of ground earth color in an oil base. They are best on darker woods with open grains such as oak or ash because they accentuate the pours. When buying commercial stains pay no attention to the name on the can. Names like golden oak, cherry or walnut can be quite deceiving. Do not even look at the names, rather look at the color chart and decide on the color you want. I once used golden oak on maple which gave the results I wanted—aged maple.

It is always best to test a stain on a scrap of wood before applying to the entire table. More and more I am electing to apply no stain at all or very light washes of aniline dye. With the former option the table can look a little anemic at completion but within six months most wood takes on a pleasing patina. Within a year it is stunning.

## USING WOOD FILLERS

On open grained woods such as walnut, oak or ash, fillers do just what the name implies. They fill the pores of the wood. Most wood fillers are padded on and the excess removed by wiping cross grain. On open grained woods a finish can be built much faster with considerably less sanding between coats if a filler is used.

# OIL FINISHES

Oil finishes are an oil which will polymerize on exposure to air, which makes it a "reactive" finish—each layer is distinct and separate from the last. Sanding between coats better enables the new coat to bond to the old. The traditional oil finish was boiled linseed oil, but today tung oil is also used extensively. Most modern oil finishes are a blend of oils with dryers added to speed the polymerization process. Oil finishes have been around for a long time, and they are what I use on many period pieces. An oil finish is low tech to apply but quite time consuming. Patience is the key and that is why my wife, Susan, does most of the oil finishing for me.

Correctly done, an oil finish can be stunning. Susan and I learned the technique below from my friend Boyd Hutchison.

# FRENCH POLISH FINISH

French polish is a method of applying shellac which is derived from a secretion of the lac bug. It is an entirely natural finish that is non-toxic and very durable. More and more it is my favorite. If a good grade of no-wax shellac is used, water can sit on it for long periods of time. As a demo, my friend Jeff Jewitt pours water on a freshly polished table and leaves it overnight, then his finishing class removes it the next morning with no harm.

The only drawback to this finish is that a wet glass will usually leave a white ring. This is usually due to using a low grade of shellac that has not been sufficiently de-waxed. It is the wax that causes the white ring. I feel this drawback is offset by the

ease of repairing French polish. A wet glass ring can usually be repaired in about ten minutes. Additionally French polish is an evaporative finish so that each new coat partially dissolves the last, and the two become one, rather than a series of separate layers, as is the case with reactive finishes such as varnish, oil, etc. (Each layer of a reactive finish is separate. This is why sanding between coats helps bonding of one to the other.) Therefore the whole piece can be spruced up every year or two with a padding of French polish.

French polish was not known before about 1820. Therefore it is not historically correct for the Queen Anne Porringer Table on page 2, even though that is what I used. I built the table for my own use so I did what I liked. The Victorians went wild over French polish because for the first time they had a really transparent tough finish. They refinished quantities of older furniture with the new process.

---

# Using Boyd's Oil Finish

## A WORD OF CAUTION

Oil finishes have a tremendous affinity for oxygen, so rags and paper soaked with oil finish are prone to spontaneous combustion. Never wad up finishing rags and wipes, as this increases the chances of spontaneous combustion. Dispose of all waste rages, wipes and paper immediately. I burn them in a wood burning stove, no matter the time of the year. If you cannot burn them, set them in a clear area outside until the oil dries and the danger of spontaneous combustion passes. Start with a commercial oil finish (buy natural, which is clear), a can of 100 percent tung oil, and a can of mineral spirits. Mix a quantity of tung oil 50 percent with mineral spirits.

**STEP 1**  Prepare the Surface
Start with the table sanded to 320 grit. Stain or fill as desired.

**STEP 2**  Apply the First Coat
Apply a coat of 90 percent oil finish mixed with 10 percent of the tung oil/mineral spirit mixture. After one hour, hand sand with 320 grit wet-dry sandpaper and wipe the excess oil away.

**STEP 3**  Apply a Second Coat
After at least twenty-four hours, apply a mixture of 80 percent finish, 20 percent Tung Oil/Mineral Spirits. After one hour, hand sand with 400-grit wet-dry sandpaper and wipe the excess oil away.

**STEP 4**  Apply the Third Coat
After at least twenty-four hours, apply a mixture of 70 percent finish, 30 percent Tung Oil/Mineral Spirits. After one hour, hand sand with 600-grit wet-dry sandpaper and wipe the excess oil away. Repeat step 4 as necessary to achieve a pleasing finish.

## FINISHING STEPS

### STEP 1

## Fill the Pores

After the first brushed coat of orange shellac has dried twenty-four hours, it is time to start the filling process. This is done with pumice powder. Dampen a pad of cheese cloth with alcohol and dip it in the pumice powder. Now rub vigorously with circular motion, going cross grain as much as possible. This will both smooth the wood and fill the pores with a mixture of shellac, pumice and wood dust. Because the pumice is damp with alcohol, it fuses with the shellac forming an effective filler. Allow to dry twenty-four hours before proceeding with the next step.

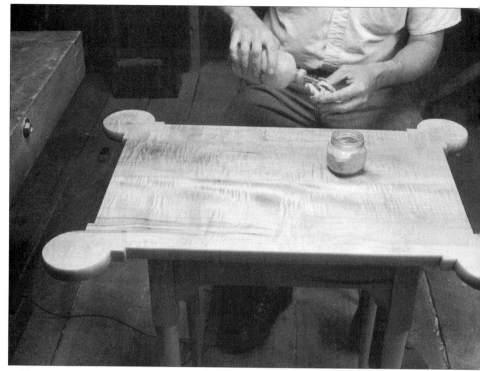

**STEP 1**

### STEP 2

## Prepare for Shellac

Saturate a piece of cotton wadding with a 1 ½ pound cut of orange shellac.

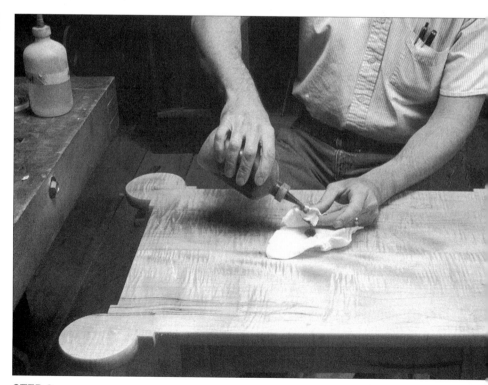

**STEP 2**

**STEP 3**

# Add Mineral Oil

Wrap the wadding in a cheese cloth cover and apply a few drops of mineral oil to the cover.

**STEP 4**

# Pad It On

Rub in a circular motion at first. The idea is to work just ahead of the tack rate of the shellac. You will see the finish start to build.

# Finish Up

Once the finish starts to build, switch to what my friend Jeff Jewitt calls "airplane strokes." You rub only with the grain, touching down and picking up on the move. The whole operation is much like an airplane doing practice landings and take-offs. Again the idea is to work just ahead of the tack rate of the shellac. Do not use too much oil; you only need a few drops to keep the pad from sticking excessively. Play with the speed of your airplane strokes until you are building finish. If the pad sticks, you are going too slow, and if you are not building finish, you are going too fast. Also play with the pressure you put on the pad; this has an effect as well.

**STEP 5**

## APPLYING A BRUSHED VARNISH FINISH

Varnish is mostly polyurethane varnish these days, and I don't like the look of it much. Still, when I need a really tough finish that can take a lot of abuse, I choose varnish. It is the finish I used on furniture for my son. A college boy's furniture needs to be "beer proof," so polyurethane is the finish of choice.

There is nothing mystical about applying varnish, simply brush it on all the while watching for runs. Sand between coats. Varnish is available in clear and semi-gloss (some manufacturers call it satin gloss). The latter is good if you desire a low luster appearance or if surface preparation was short and sweet. I prefer to use gloss and steel wool the final coat if a semi-gloss finish is what I desire. Varnish is available at any hardware store.

# USING WATER BASED FINISHES

Water based finishes are becoming more and more popular. This is largely for environmental reasons. Disposing of oil based products can be harmful to the environment. It is also why I am turning back to shellac, the alcohol causes few environmental problems.

I have not yet found a water based finish that I think equals shellac or oil based finishes. Great progress is being made, however, and I am sure we will see finishes that are equal. They may exist now, I just have not found one.

## APPLYING A MILK PAINT FINISH

Milk paint is a finish I use frequently on utility tables. It is the finish I used on the dining table for this table was built to go on our screen porch. The screen porch adjoins our kitchen where a dining table built for us by Kelly Mehler is. I wanted the porch table to mimic the style of Kelly's table but used a painted finish because it better resists weather. This is also why I did not put a drawer in the table.

Milk paint has been used for centuries and can be made at home by mixing equal parts of powdered milk, quick lime and ground color. I buy my milk paint from The Old Fashioned Milk Paint Co. I mix it with water according to the directions and apply two to three coats to a well prepared surface. I allow one hour minimum between coats. After the final coat has dried for twenty-four hours I steel wool lightly then brush on a coat of Minwax Antique Oil Finish and wipe away the excess. Boiled linseed oil was used in Colonial times and can still be used today. A drying oil is necessary over the milk paint as a fixative. Milk paint gives a very durable (it is unstripable) pleasing finish that wears gracefully. Antiquing can be instant by steel wooling the edges that would normally wear fast.

## GENERAL

American Association
of Woodturners
3200 Lexington Avenue
Shoreview, MN 55126
Information on
woodturning.

Airstream Dust Helmets
Hwy 54 South
PO Box 975
Elbow Lake, MN 56531
Safety and dust protection
equipment.

Conover Workshops
PO Box 679
Parkman, OH 44080
E-mail: ERConover@aol.com

L. & J.G. Stickley, Inc.
Stickley Drive
PO Box 480
Manluis, NY 13104-0408
The present day company
founded by the Stickley brothers.
Their catalog is $10 and well
worth the price for anyone
building Craftsman style
furniture.

## WOOD

Adams Wood Products L.P.
974 Forest Drive
Morristown, TN 37814
Many styles of legs in a
variety of woods.

Badger Hardwoods of Wisconsin
N 1517 Highway 14
Walworth, WI 53184
Seventeen hardwood species
available kiln dried and in
sizes from 4/4 to 12/4.

Bristol Valley Hardwoods
4300 Bristol Valley Road
Canadaigua, NY 14424
Many different species
of hardwood.

Catskill Mountain Lumber
PO Box 450
Swan Lake, NY 12783
Wide variety of dimensioned,
dried lumber.

Colonial Hardwoods, Inc.
7953 Cameron Brown Ct.
Springfield, VA 22153
Over 120 species of hardwoods
available 1/4" to 4" thick.

Constantine's
2050 Eastchester Rd
Bronx, NY 10461
Carries veneer, hardware
and supplies.

Crafter's Mart
PO Box 2342
Greeley, CO 80632
Wide variety of wood turnings.

Cupboard Distributing
114 South Main Street
Urbana, OH 43078
Small wooden products such
as knobs, pulls and pins as
well as other supplies.

Eagle Woodworking, Inc.
1130 East Street
Tewksbury, MA 01876
Custom-made dovetailed
maple drawers.

Frank Paxton Lumber Company
6311 St. John Avenue
Kansas City, MO 64123
Offers many services plus
50 exotic woods and a variety
of domestic species.

MacBeath Hardwood
930 Ashby Avenue
Berkeley, CA 94710
Extensive product list in both
exotic and domestic species.

Matthew Burak Furniture
PO Box 279
Danville, VT 05828
Grain-matched and mortised legs in
various styles, sizes and woods.

Niagara Lumber & Wood
Products, Inc.
47 Elm Street
East Aurora, NY 14052
Specializes in northern
Appalachian hardwoods.

Rainbow Woods
20 Andrews Street
Newman, GA 30263
Wide variety of hardwood turnings.

Scherr's Cabinets
5315 Burdic Expressway East
Rt. 5, Box 12
Minot, ND
Custom-made drawer fronts in a
wide variety of woods.

Tatro, Inc.
7011 Marcelle Street
Paramount, CA
Various wood turnings and shapes.

Tropical Exotic Hardwoods
PO Box 1806
Carlsbad, CA 92018
Imports a wide variety of exotic
woods available in sizes up
through 8/4.

## HARDWARE

Antique Hardware Store
RD 2 Box A
Kintnersville, PA 18930
Features cast iron and brass hard-
ware such as pulls and knobs.

Horton Brasses, Inc.
Nooks Hill Road
Cromwell, CT 06416
Furniture hardware such as pulls,
knobs, hinges and casters made
of brass, wood, porcelain and
hand-forged iron.

Paxton Hardware
7818 Bradshaw Road
PO Box 256
Upper Falls, MD 21156
Wide line of period furniture
hardware in brass and iron.

Stanley Hardware
480 Myrtle Street
New Britain, CT 06053
Full line of hardware,
including brass.

Wayne's Woods, Inc.
39 North Plains Industrial Road
Wallingford, CT 06492
Specializes in brass, glass, porcelain
and wood reproduction hardware.

Whitechapel, Ltd
3650 Highway 22
PO Box 136
Wilson, WY 83014
Hardware, especially solid brass and
wrought iron period hardware.

Woodcraft Supply Corp.
5300 Briscoe Road
PO Box 1686
Parkersburg, WV 26102
Carries hardware, tools
and supplies.

Woodworker's Hardware
PO Box 784
St. Cloud, MN 56302
Lists more than 4,000 pieces of
hardware including pulls, drawer
slides and reproduction pieces.

Woodworker's Store
21801 Industrial Boulevard
Rogers, MN 55374-9514
Wide line of hardware including
knobs and knockdown fasteners.

Woodworkers Store
4365 Willow Drive
Medina, MN 55340
A very complete line of general
hardware, especially specialty items
such as knock-down hardware,
metal drawer slides, etc.

## TOOLS

A&I Supply
401 Radio City Drive
North Pekin, IL 61554
Variety of woodworking tools and
equipment at discount prices.

Amana Tool Corporation
120 Carolyn Boulevard
Farmingdale, NY 11375
Manufactures industrial-grade,
carbide-tipped woodcutting tools
including router bits, planer knives,
and saw blades.

DeRose & Company
Box 150 Hanover Green Drive
Mechanicsville, VA 23111
Manufactures custom lathes.

Eagle America Corporation
PO Box 1099
Chardon, OH 44024
Large selection of router bits
and other tools and supplies.

Eastwood Company
580 Lancaster Avenue
Malvern, PA 19355
Although mostly automotive, carries
many specialty and unusual tools.

Hartville Tool and Supply
940 West Maple Street
Hartville, IN 44632
Many woodworking tools
and accessories.

Highland Hardware
1045 N. Highland
Atlanta, GA 30306
Carries a variety of woodworking
tools and hardware.

Klein Design, Inc.
17910 Southeast 110th Street
Renton, WA 98059
Produces lathes as well as tools
and accessories for them.

Kreg Tool Company
PO Box 367
201 Campus Drive
Huxley, IA 50124
Produces jigs and other
woodworking supplies.

Leigh Industries, Ltd.
PO Box 357
Port Coquitlam, B.C. V3C 4K6
Canada
Carries a number of dovetail jigs.

Lie-Nielsen Toolworks
Route 1
Warren, ME 04684
High quality hand tools,
including planes.

MLCS, Ltd.
PO Box 4053C13
Rydal, PA 19046
Carries a wide variety of router bits.

Nemy Electric Tool Company
7635-A Auburn Boulevard
Citrus Heights, CA 95610
Offers many tools to woodworkers
of all levels.

Penn State Industries
2850 Comly Road
Philadelphia, PA 19154
Variety of woodworking machines
for the hobbyist.

Ridge Carbide Tool Corporation
PO Box 497
595 York Avenue
Lyndhurst, NJ 07071
Makes custom router bits, shaper
knives, saw blades, and dado sets.

Taylor Design Group
PO Box 810262
Dallas, TX 75381
Maker of Incra jigs as well as a
number of other woodworking
accessories.

Vermont-American Tool Company
PO Box 340
Lincolnton, NC  28093-0340
Manufactures a full line of bits,
blades and specialty tools.

Whiteside Machine Company
4506 Shook Road
Claremont, NC  28610
Manufactures large line of carbide
and carbide-tipped router bits.

Windsor Forge
1403 Harlem Boulevard
Rockford, IL  61103
Blacksmith shop that produces
eighteenth and nineteenth century
hand tools, particularly
carving tools.

## FINISHING

Amazon Lumber & Trading
Corporation, Ltd.
PO Box 530156
Miami Shores, FL  33153
Makes a variety of oil finishes.

The Old Fashion Milk Paint Co.
Main Street
Groton, MA  01450
Manufactures milk paint.

# INDEX

# More Great Books For Your Woodshop!

**Marvelous Wooden Boxes You Can Make**—Master woodworker Jeff Greef offers plans for 20 beautiful, functional boxes, complete with drawings, cutting lists, numbered step-by-step instructions and color photographs. *#70287/$24.99/144 pages/67 color, 225 b&w illus.*

**Good Wood Joints**—Learn which joints are best for specific situations and how to skillfully make them. You'll discover joints for every application, the basics of joint cutting and much more! Plus, you'll find an ingenious chart that makes choosing the right joint for the job easy. All well-illustrated with step-by-step instructions for making joinery by machine or hand. *#70313/$19.99/128 pages/550 color illus.*

**Getting the Very Best from Your Scroll Saw**—You'll turn to this technique, pattern and project book to learn how to get professional-quality results every time. You'll get directions on it all from cutting dovetails to cutting metal to creating inlays, marquetry and intarsia mosaics. You'll discover how to make puzzles, gifts, games, toys, Victorian fretwork shelves, moldings and much more! *#70289/$19.99/160 pages/200 b&w illus./paperback*

**Make Your Own Jigs & Woodshop Furniture**—Innovative jigs and fixtures will help you specialize your ordinary power tools without spending big money. You'll get plans for over 40 jigs and fixtures, 23 projects for a well-outfitted workshop and more! *#70249/$24.99/144 pages/100 b&w, 100 color illus.*

**Making Wooden Mechanical Models**—Discover plans for 15 handsome and incredibly clever machines with visible wheels, cranks, pistons and other moving parts made of wood. Expertly photographed and complete with materials lists and diagrams, the plans call for a challenging variety of techniques and procedures. *#70288/$21.99/144 pages/341 illus./paperback*

**Good Wood Handbook**—Your guide to selecting and using the right wood for the job (before you buy). You'll see a wide selection of commercial softwoods and hardwoods in full color. *#70162/$16.99/128 pages/250+ color illus.*

**Display Cabinets You Can Customize**—Go beyond building to designing furniture. You'll receive step-by-step instructions to the base projects—the starting points for a wide variety of pieces, such as display cabinets, tables and cases. Then you'll learn about customizing techniques. You'll see how to adapt a glass front cabinet, put a profile on a cabinet by using molding, get a different look by using stained glass, changing the legs and much more! *#70282/$18.99/128 pages/150 b&w illus./paperback*

**Blizzard's Book of Woodworking**—Step-by-step demonstrations for a wide range of projects for home and garden will hone your skills and improve your technique. *#70163/$22.95/208 pages/350+ b&w, 30 color illus.*

**Pocket Guide to Wood Finishes**—This handy guide gives you instant visual guidance for mixing stains and other finishes. Spiral bound and durable—perfect for your woodshop. *#70164/$16.95/64 pages/200+ color illus.*

**Build Your Own Mobile Power Tool Centers**—Learn how to-"expand" shop space by building mobile workstations that maximize utility, versatility and accessibility of woodshop tools and accessories. *#70283/$19.99/144 pages/250 b&w illus./paperback*

**Creating Your Own Woodshop**—Discover dozens of economical ways to fill unused space with the woodshop of your dreams. Self shows you how to convert space, layout the ideal woodshop, or improve your existing shop. *#70229/$18.99/128 pages/162 b&w photos/illus./paperback*

**Building Fine Furniture from Solid Wood**—You'll build beautiful wood furniture with 11 of Sadler's most popular projects complete with instructions, exploded drawings and detailed photographs. *#70230/$24.95/160 pages/175 b&w, 35 color illus.*

**How To Sharpen Every Blade in Your Woodshop**—You know that tools perform best when razor sharp—yet you avoid the dreaded chore. This ingenious guide brings you plans for jigs and devices that make sharpening any blade short and simple! Includes jigs for sharpening boring tools, router bits and more! *#70250/$17.99/144 pages/157 b&w illus./paperback*

**The Woodworker's Sourcebook, 2nd Edition**—Shop for woodworking supplies from home! Self has compiled listings for everything from books and videos to plans and associations. Each listing has an address and telephone number and is rated in terms of quality and price. *#70281/$19.99/160 pages/50 illus.*

**Basic Woodturning Techniques**—Detailed explanations of fundamental techniques like faceplate and spindle turning will have you turning beautiful pieces in no time. *#70211/$14.95/112 pages/119 b&w illus./paperback*

**Woodworker's Guide to Pricing Your Work**—Turn your hobby into profit! You'll find out how other woodworkers set their prices and sell their products. You'll learn how to estimate average materials cost per project, increase your income without sacrificing quality or enjoyment, build repeat and referral business, manage a budget and much more! *#70268/$18.99/160 pages/paperback*

**Measure Twice Cut Once**—Achieve good proportion, clean cuts and snug fits every time! You'll learn what each measuring tool does, how to use it properly—even how to make your own. *#70210/$18.99/128 pages/143 illus./paperback*

**The Stanley Book of Woodworking Tools, Techniques and Projects**—Become a better woodworker by mastering the fundamentals of choosing the right wood, cutting tight fitting joints, properly using a marking gauge and much more. *#70264/$19.95/160 pages/400 color illus./paperback*

**Woodworker's Guide to Selecting and Milling Wood**—Save money on lumber as you preserve the great tradition of felling, milling and drying your own wood. Loads of full-color illustrations will help you identify the right wood for every job. *#70248/$22.99/144 pages/128 b&w illus., 32 color photos*

**Make Your Woodworking Pay for Itself**—Find simple hints for selling your work to pay for shop improvements or generate a little extra income! *#10323/$16.99/128 pages/30 b&w illus./paperback*